Managing Modern Youth Work

L

Titles in the Series

To order, please contact our distributor: BEBC Distribution, Albion Close, Parkstone, Poole BH12 3LL. Telephone: 0845 230 9000, email: **learningmatters@bebc.co.uk.** You can also find more information on each of these titles and our other learning resources at **www.learningmatters.co.uk.**

Managing Modern Youth Work

MARY TYLER, LIZ HOGGARTH AND BRYAN MERTON

Series Editors: Janet Batsleer and Keith Popple

LearningMatters

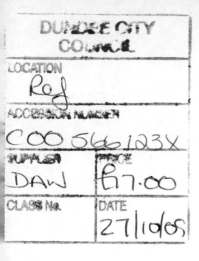
First published in 2009 by Learning Matters Ltd

British Library Cataloguing in Publication Data

A CIP record for this book is available from the British Library.

ISBN 978 1 84445 206 4

Cover and text design by Code 5 Design Associates Ltd
Project management by Swales & Willis
Typeset by Swales & Willis, Exeter, Devon
Printed and bound in Great Britain by TJ International Ltd, Padstow, Cornwall

Learning Matters Ltd
33 Southernhay East
Exeter EX1 1NX
Tel: 01392 215560
info@learningmatters.co.uk
www.learningmatters.co.uk

FSC
Mixed Sources
Product group from well-managed
forests and other controlled sources
Cert no. SGS-COC-2482
www.fsc.org
© 1996 Forest Stewardship Council

This book is dedicated to David Batchelor and Malcolm Payne who both retire from De Montfort University at the time of its publication. We wish to recognise their huge contribution to the education and training of professional youth and community workers and to the development of practitioner and academic research and writing on youth and community work during their careers.

Contents

Foreword from the Series Editors

Youth work and community work has a long, rich and diverse history that spans three centuries. The development of youth work extends from the late nineteenth and early twentieth century with the emergence of voluntary groups and the serried ranks of the UK's many uniformed youth organisations, through to modern youth club work, youth project work and informal education. Youth work remains in the early twenty-first century a mixture of voluntary effort and paid and state sponsored activity.

Community work also had its beginnings in voluntary activity. Some of this activity was in the form of 'rescuing the poor', whilst community action developed as a response to oppressive circumstances and was based on the idea of self-help. In the second half of the twentieth century the state financed a good deal of local authority and government sponsored community and regeneration work and now there are multi-various community action projects and campaigns.

Today there are thousands of people involved in youth work and community work both in paid positions and in voluntary roles. However, the activity is undergoing significant change. National Occupation Standards and a new academic benchmarking statement have recently been introduced and soon all youth and community workers undertaking qualifying courses and who successfully graduate will do so with an honours degree.

Empowering Youth and Community Work Practice is a series of texts primarily aimed at students on youth and community work courses. However, more experienced practitioners from a wide range of fields will find these books useful because they offer effective ways of integrating theory, knowledge and practice. Written by experienced lecturers, practitioners and policy commentators each title covers core aspects of what is needed to be an effective practitioner and will address key competences for professional JNC recognition as a youth and community worker. The books use case studies, activities and references to the latest government initiatives to help readers learn and develop their theoretical understanding and practice. This series then will provide invaluable support to anyone studying or practising in the field of youth and community work as well as a number of other related fields.

Janet Batsleer
Manchester Metropolitan University

Keith Popple
London South Bank University

Chapter 1

Introduction

Mary Tyler

Rationale for the book

When people set out to qualify in youth work, they are keen to develop their understanding of young people and their skills to work with them. They do not generally anticipate that they will also need to learn about managing – managing themselves; aims, intentions and outcomes; activities and projects; learning experiences and environments; budgets; volunteers and staff. Perhaps most important of these responsibilities is managing themselves – if youth workers cannot do this, then young people will lose out. They also have to manage the educational opportunities and processes they create otherwise young people's learning and enjoyment will be limited by this. They must manage the other people whose role is to contribute to these processes or else projects will flounder. This book takes a positive approach encouraging workers to feel and to be able to be in charge, rather than feel like victims at the mercy of the world. What can be more rewarding than knowing you are responsible for successful responsive youth work which is making a positive difference to young people's lives?

Whilst developing skills as effective informal educators, the youth worker in training and the recently qualified professional are also building the necessary management skills and this book is designed to play a part in that. These skills are initially focused on the worker but steadily become integrated into the wider range of responsibilities that the emerging professional undertakes. Those experienced workers who move into roles with more management responsibility can use this book to review these skills and add to them using the practical information, advice and discussion offered.

The book starts from the youth worker at the hub and their relationship with their immediate environment and what they can control and influence. Then, chapter by chapter, it progresses outward from the hub towards the edges of the circle in the direction of government policy and its implications. At each step outwards the worker is enabled to develop an understanding of this widening world; their position and power; who judges the work they are responsible for; what is involved in managing others to do that work; how they can extend their influence; and what they can achieve. Workers will also increasingly recognise their managerial position: facing towards youth work funding and the policies driving it while simultaneously facing in the other direction towards young people and others in the communities with whom they work.

This book aims to achieve this developmental journey by providing plenty of practical advice and illustration of the operational (day to day) and strategic (longer term) work managers of youth work have to be able to handle competently. It uses a number of questions and activities to help the reader's reflection and learning process. Earlier chapters are directed more at those new to thinking about and taking management responsibility. The later chapters are designed more for experienced workers and managers. The earlier chapters include more theory than later chapters as they have a scene-setting role but this is not a textbook about management theory. It is a book about how to do it. There are suggestions for further reading at the end of each chapter. An outline of each chapter is provided at the end of this introduction.

This first chapter is designed to set the scene by considering the extent to which professional youth work involves management work. It identifies what management work comprises, looking at the range of responsibilities and tasks and their balance depending on the grade and level at which you are employed and in what kind of work context. It also provides an introduction to some management theory by looking at a model of management roles and a broad definition of management. Ideas about management that are taken for granted are challenged by contrasting briefly the positivist and interpretivist perspectives in order to engage you as a critically reflective practitioner and thinker about management. It briefly sets out the current context of youth work in England and argues that it is even more essential than before that youth work is well managed.

National Occupational Standards

At the beginning of each chapter in this book the relevant occupational standards for youth work will be identified to help you clarify potential learning outcomes. These were published early in 2008 and represent the latest agreed 'range of functions undertaken across youth work, across the public and voluntary sectors' (LLUK, 2008, Appendix 2). The main functions and principal areas of activity are listed in Figure 1.1 (see p3). The full set of standards is available from the Lifelong Learning website (www.lluk.org.uk). There is no assumption that any one youth worker will be doing all this. This book is clearly concerned mainly with the management activities (significantly functions 4 and 5), more of which will obviously be undertaken by those with specific management responsibilities although many of the activities are seen to be interrelated.

Management as a reality of modern youth work

Students' knowledge and understanding of youth work as they enter professional training is often based almost entirely on face-to-face work. However, the reality is that the full-time professional worker may well spend no more than 50 per cent of their time face to face with young people depending on the nature of their role.

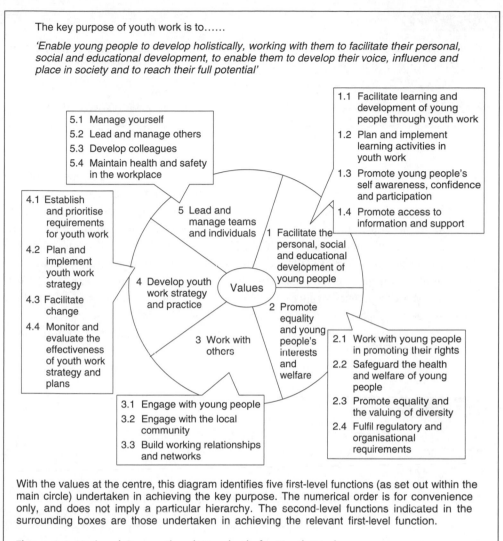

The key purpose of youth work is to......

'Enable young people to develop holistically, working with them to facilitate their personal, social and educational development, to enable them to develop their voice, influence and place in society and to reach their full potential'

5.1 Manage yourself
5.2 Lead and manage others
5.3 Develop colleagues
5.4 Maintain health and safety in the workplace

1.1 Facilitate learning and development of young people through youth work
1.2 Plan and implement learning activities in youth work
1.3 Promote young people's self awareness, confidence and participation
1.4 Promote access to information and support

4.1 Establish and prioritise requirements for youth work
4.2 Plan and implement youth work strategy
4.3 Facilitate change
4.4 Monitor and evaluate the effectiveness of youth work strategy and plans

5 Lead and manage teams and individuals

1 Facilitate the personal, social and educational development of young people

4 Develop youth work strategy and practice

Values

2 Promote equality and young people's interests and welfare

3 Work with others

2.1 Work with young people in promoting their rights
2.2 Safeguard the health and welfare of young people
2.3 Promote equality and the valuing of diversity
2.4 Fulfil regulatory and organisational requirements

3.1 Engage with young people
3.2 Engage with the local community
3.3 Build working relationships and networks

With the values at the centre, this diagram identifies five first-level functions (as set out within the main circle) undertaken in achieving the key purpose. The numerical order is for convenience only, and does not imply a particular hierarchy. The second-level functions indicated in the surrounding boxes are those undertaken in achieving the relevant first-level function.

Figure 1.1 National Occupational Standards for Youth Work

Source: LLUK, 2008

Youth workers have to gather data about and get to know the neighbourhoods they work in and the groups of young people who are their key focus. They may also need to research need; plan both alone and with colleagues; prepare funding bids; book minibuses and order stationery; attend meetings in and beyond their organisations; recruit, manage and supervise staff and volunteers; collate and input monitoring data; and write reports. This activity is not face-to-face youth work. Some of this is administration but most of it is management work. We will look at definitions of management later in this chapter under the section 'The meaning of management'.

ACTIVITY 1.1

- *What do youth workers do in their capacity as managers of youth work? Depending on your level of experience and responsibility, list the activities you do, or observe others do, which could be described as management.*

- *How do you feel about the nature of this work and taking responsibility for it?*

The amount of management work youth workers undertake and its range depends on the grade at which they are employed. The national JNC employer–staff agreement used by a wide range of youth work employers states that an experienced 'youth and community support worker' in England and Wales will 'deliver operational youth and community support work in local and area projects' (JNC, 2007, Appendix 2). Anyone employed at the 'professional range' (qualified at higher education level or the equivalent) will 'carry strategic and operational responsibility for service delivery, design and development' (JNC, 2007, Appendix 2). The competence needed 'involves the application of knowledge and skills in a broad range of complex, technical or professional work activities performed in a wide variety of contexts, with a substantial degree of personal responsibility and autonomy' (JNC, 2007, Appendix 2).

ACTIVITY 1.2

Read this list taken from the Joint Negotiating Committee for Youth and Community Workers guidance on allocation to ranges (JNC, 2007, Appendix 1: 1–2). Which of these duties do you identify as management tasks?

Example of key duties for the youth and community support worker.

- *Working directly with young people to develop their social education by providing programmes of activities, services and facilities.*

- *Establishing contact with and guiding young people as part of local programmes.*

- *Providing advice and support to local community groups and agencies.*

- *Assisting in the motivation, retention, developing and support of staff and volunteers.*

- *Contributing to service development by planning, delivering and monitoring of local provisions.*

- *Implementing equal opportunities policies.*

- *Establishing and maintaining relationships with young people and community groups.*

- *Maintaining quality of service provision including giving directions to other workers.*

ACTIVITY *1.2* *continued*

- *First line management responsibility for workers and volunteers, including recruiting, developing and initial disciplining of staff.*

- *Initiating and monitoring developments of services, particularly with other agencies.*

- *Performing and ensuring the discharge of administrative duties (including budget control, records keeping and health and safety).*

Example of key duties for professional range.

- *Performing all the duties for youth and community support workers.*

- *Managing and developing a range of services.*

- *Managing and developing staff and facilities.*

- *Working with other agencies to develop services across the community.*

- *Design, lead and implement a youth work curriculum.*

- *Leading project development and implementation.*

Management responsibilities and roles

Your management responsibilities will vary according to not only your grade but also the context. All youth workers are responsible for the quality of their own work and are accountable formally to their employing organisation and their manager and informally to young people. Many are responsible for one or more projects too so they have to manage, for instance, budgets, equipment, buildings and other staff and volunteers. This contrasts with the circumstances of some other professionals who work with young people who are clearly responsible just for managing their own workload.

The type of management responsibility you carry is also dependent on the level where you are sited in the organisation hierarchy. The higher up the organisation, the more strategic responsibility you have and the more time you spend in decision making but the more you are dependent on those you manage for information to understand what is happening at service delivery level. If you work in a local community delivering youth work for the local authority or a voluntary organisation, then local adults, young people and part-time staff and volunteers will tend to see you as the leader as well as the manager and may expect you to be able to make decisions that you do not have the authority to make. Although some of these stakeholders will understand that you are an employee of a larger organisation, others will need to learn this from you.

Typically as a youth work professional you have to provide leadership as well as ensure things are ticking over. A simple and commonly used distinction between leadership and management is that the first is about providing strategic direction, *what the organisation is for*, and the second is about coordination of a set of activities, *what it does*, to achieve that direction.

There are many ways of understanding the range of roles and tasks of the manager. Sandy Adirondack looks at managers in the voluntary sector. Her diagram of 'What managers do' (2006, p3) places the core work of the organisation, in this case youth work, at the hub of a wheel of management categories since managers in small agencies and projects are also involved in direct delivery to their service users. She then categorises the day to day or operational management which fills in the spokes of the wheel:

- manage the work;

- manage the people who do the work;

- manage information and communication;

- manage external communication;

- manage finance;

- manage material resources.

Around the tyre of the wheel, and therefore encompassing all this work, is the governance and strategic management which includes all the bigger picture and longer-term visioning and planning, decision making and responsibility.

Quinn et al. (2007) provide a more analytical way of understanding and categorising the roles and tasks of managers, informed by a range of theories and models of management that have been developed over more than a hundred years. Many of these models such as the rational goal with its emphasis on efficiency and the open systems model with its emphasis on flexibility are explained in management textbooks (e.g. Mullins, 2007; Watson, 2006; Grey, 2009) and we look further at some of these models in Chapter 4. Quinn (2007, p16) identifies eight key roles such as that of 'coordinator' which are shaded in Figure 1.2 and paired in four quadrants. Each of these quadrants reflects the key interests and concerns of one influential management model, each of which has a greater or lesser emphasis on flexibility *or* control and on the internal *or* external aspects of the organisation. He argues that we use all these roles at different times despite their being housed in different quadrants.

To the developing professional this range of roles and responsibilities can feel pretty daunting. You could feel this will be too much to cope with and so there is a danger that this could become a self-fulfilling prophecy. It is important therefore to realise the relevance and value of the key life skills that you have already, such as dealing with conflict between your siblings or your children at home (facilitator role), or your ability to solve problems in previous jobs by coming up with new solutions (innovator role). These skills

> ### ACTIVITY *1.3*
>
> - *What kinds of overlaps can you identify between any of these generic management roles in Figure 1.2 and those you undertake as a youth worker?*
>
> - *How do you feel about each of these management roles?*
>
> - *Which ones are you more confident about and which do you feel least prepared for and why?*

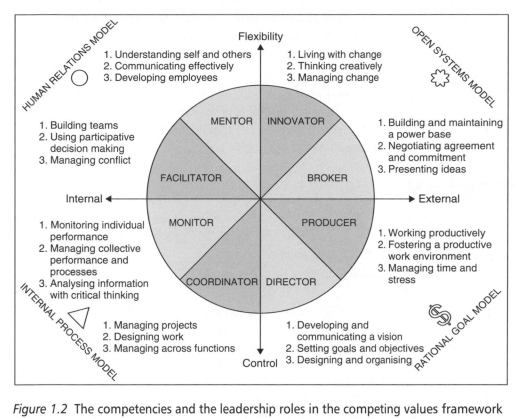

Figure 1.2 The competencies and the leadership roles in the competing values framework

Note: Each of the eight leadership roles in the competing values framework contains three competencies. They, like the value, both complement the ones next to them and contrast with those opposite to them.

Source: Quinn, 2007, p48; reproduced with permission of John Wiley & Sons, Inc.

can be applied in your new professional circumstances and you can seek help, advice and training for those skills you need to develop.

The meaning of management

There is plenty of debate about the meaning of management (e.g. Mullins, 2007; Watson, 2006) but 'the art of getting things done through people' is a commonly used very simple explanation. It was apparently coined by Mary Parker Follett (1868–1933), a management theorist, radical in her time, who was originally involved in community education (Smith, 2002). She applied her focus on the human element of management at a time when classical and scientific management theories were prominent which focused mainly on structure and mechanics (Coulshed and Mullender, 2006).

Tony Watson, a social scientist who has studied current managers' views of their work and its effects on their lives, offers a definition that develops this explanation of management further and indicates some of the complexity associated with it.

The overall shaping of relationships, understandings and processes within a work organisation to bring about the completion of the tasks undertaken in the organisation's name in such a way that the organisation continues into the future.

(Watson, 2006, p167)

He also argues (2001, p44) that managers both develop and express their identity and individuality through the way they act and think in their managerial work and how they help to 'shape' their organisations. So we can see that the meaning we give our work as a manager is personal and therefore different for each of us.

ACTIVITY **1.4**

Do you understand management as something that comes naturally to some of us and not others, or do you think it is a set of knowledge and skills that anyone can learn and improve? Discuss this question with another worker.

Clearly management involves creativity as tricky judgements have to be made for which in most cases there is no one right answer. For instance, when and in what way do you raise concerns with your administrative worker about how they are performing so that you can have a constructive discussion rather than simply upset them (see Chapter 4 for advice on such circumstances)? Management also involves employing proven techniques, applying competence based on training and experience. For instance, there is plenty of guidance and training about developing a clear job description and person specification and using these to structure interview questions when recruiting staff (see Chapter 4). Conventional learning about organisations and management is very appealing but can lead students to assume there are more 'certainties' (Grey, 2009, p170) than is the reality. Such learning can also tend to ignore the richness of organisational study through its somewhat formulaic approach to management activity.

We cannot consider what management means without considering power. Youth work places values about social justice and tackling oppression at its centre. It is work with a strong ethical base that is concerned about the rights and capacities of young people rather than a deficit model that assumes young people are lacking and problematic (Batsleer, 2008, p21). There is also a very strong emphasis on engaging young people in decision making at all levels in and beyond youth work settings.

There is a risk that this commitment to empowerment can lead you to believe that in your role as professional worker with responsibilities for staff and volunteers you must behave as if you are all equal in the team. The reality is that you carry more power as this is integral to the responsible role you have as the professional worker (and possibly labelled as manager too). If you ignore or play down this 'position' power, you also ignore this responsibility which means there is a serious risk that either it is not being carried properly or you are leaving others who are probably less qualified than you to pick up some of this responsibility. In either case the end result could lead to some poor and potentially oppressive management practice.

If you do not shoulder your responsibility, second-rate youth work practice could become the norm. If you do not raise minor issues about practice with staff because you are reluctant to take responsibility, and potentially to have to handle some conflict, then that practice could deteriorate. Doing nothing in such circumstances means you are condoning poor practice. Such power and responsibility is necessary to ensure your team are doing good youth work so you need to understand it. A fuller understanding of power can reduce the risk that it will be abused. Sharing power and empowering staff and volunteers is a sensitive, skilled, positive and purposeful business. This leadership aspect of management responsibilities draws on the same principles as those of youth work – it should mirror the values and the kinds of responsibilities youth workers take in supporting, developing and empowering young people. As a manager of staff it is important that you are friendly in your style, but your purpose is not to be a friend. (See Chapter 4 for a fuller discussion about such aspects of managing staff.)

So management is complex and demanding, but how important is it in the wider scheme of things? Its potential to make a difference depends on whose meaning or perspective you consider. However, from the 1970s in the UK successive governments have seen better management as a way of solving many problems they have to tackle. The thinking might be characterised as *if we can just get the organisational structures right and the 'superman/woman'* (as summarised by Pollitt, 2003) *and their methods in place, we can transform public services*.

This perspective is based on a positivist approach to management, commonly called managerialism, which believes in and seeks scientific explanations and solutions for managing organisations and their work. It has been much criticised (Grey, 2009; Haynes, 2003). Often the methods and structures government valued were those from the commercial profit-making sector, which was seen to be more effective than the public sector. Yet many of the services which government is responsible for funding are based on decisions about policy which are driven by politics not profit. This means effectiveness of those services is judged not by the profits made but by a range of potentially conflicting criteria such as meeting need, maintaining individual and public safety and producing educated and self-motivated young citizens at a reasonable cost. These criteria all have to be trickily balanced by those who manage public services and who are ultimately responsible to politicians and citizens not shareholders (see Haynes, 2003, Chapter 1 for a very helpful discussion about this). Therefore we must recognise the value of the improved accountability and the need for evidencing our achievements in youth work that managerialism has brought and at the same time be critical about its tendency to distort our focus too much towards targets and measurement.

Learning about management and organisations 'matters' as Grey says because 'it is fundamentally about the world we want to live in' (2009, p19). It is about values and therefore about a commitment not only to doing things right but also to doing the right thing. Given that management is so important, we need to become critical managers. What we mean by this is that you need a critical mind to inform you as you go. You need to be as much a critically reflective practitioner in your management work as in your face-to-face youth and community work. You need to keep asking questions of yourself and others. For instance, why this policy, why this kind of organisation, why this way of doing things?

What's really going on? Who made that decision and why? What other ways can we manage this? How do I feel about this work I am responsible for? Is it youth work I am being asked to manage or something else?

Managing modern youth work – why now?

Since the Labour government from 1997 concerned itself with tackling social exclusion and young people and developed policies which recognised youth work's contribution, youth workers have increasingly been expected to perform and meet policy targets like those working in other modern public services. Well-managed youth work is seen as part of the solution to society's concerns about young people. Whatever we may feel about any more negative managerialist aspects of this, it is essential now for the survival of youth work that professionally qualified youth workers employed in the public and voluntary sector at all levels engage in effective management of projects, finance and staff and also practise good youth work. In England much of professional youth work is now part of inter-disciplinary Children and Young People's Services or is commissioned by them and contributes to many multi-agency partnerships, so youth workers also have to manage work undertaken in a variety of settings with many partners. (See Chapters 7 and 8 respectively for more detailed explanation and discussion about partnerships, and youth work and policy.)

As this book is written we find ourselves in a time of flux in terms of organisational structures in services for children and young people and the potential impact on youth work could be positive or negative. Most important is the impact on youth work's contribution to meeting young people's interests and needs which could be compromised (Davies and Merton, 2009) and that it 'retains its focus on education, enjoyment and informality' (OFSTED, 2009, p6).

Youth work's hallmark has always been its provision of open access, non-stigmatised and often very local opportunities and services for young people. However, it has now been drawn more and more formally into the mainstream of services 'helping' those defined as in need. This has happened as a result of English policy developed through *Every Child Matters* (DfES, 2003), through *Youth Matters* (DfES, 2005) and more recently the ten-year Aiming Higher agenda (DCSF, 2007) (see Chapter 8 for more information). There have been pros and cons to its changing position. Youth work has increased its credibility, visibility and accountability, but may have reduced its creativity and flexibility about the nature of the work and about which young people it is expected to target, more of whom are now formally identified or referred.

Modern youth work takes place in and youth workers are employed by an ever-increasing range of organisations. You may be working, for instance, in a multi-disciplinary team or co-located within the local authority; for a voluntary organisation commissioned by the local authority to provide a range of youth work services; in a school; for a church, temple, synagogue or mosque providing youth work and community development activities for young people in its membership and the local community; with an organisational or area-wide responsibility, for instance, for youth forums; or for the NHS in a sexual health or drug action team, or a hospital. There is a growing trend therefore for youth workers not to be housed with other youth work colleagues and/or to be managed by professionals who are not youth workers.

Consequently it is even more essential than before that you are confident about youth work's contribution and how to manage it so its distinctive informal style and processes continue in this complex integrated world. This means you must take on your leadership role about direction, values and purpose as much as the management role about coordination of a set of activities. So there is a great need now for a focus on and advice about the specifics of managing modern youth work. This book is designed to play a part.

Outline of chapters

Now that this first chapter has set the scene, the subsequent chapters consider many key facets of managing modern youth work.

Chapter 2 focuses on you and your work patterns and discusses ways of taking control of these, building your confidence, competence and clarity in your professional role. This role is placed in the context of the complex world in which we work and you are reminded of the importance of youth work values as your guide. These values should inform your priorities when managing your time. Practical tips are provided about time management, something most workers struggle with regularly. Then we consider how you work with the wide range of other people youth workers necessarily are in contact with, focusing on communication and how you present yourself. This includes how professional youth workers and managers communicate from a place in between the workers 'at the coalface' and those managing the organisation as a whole.

Chapter 3 pursues the theme of working in the context of an employing organisation. It starts with a brief look at competing perspectives on organisations, which helps you develop your ability to think critically about them and your management. The interrelated concepts of structure and culture are used to analyse organisations you know and some hypothetical case studies of organisations which deliver youth work. You are also introduced to other models to help you understand your organisation and its youth work. These models can additionally enable you to question and evaluate in order to improve youth work's quality and responsiveness to change in the external environment.

Chapters 4 to 6 concentrate mainly on the internal environment and look in turn at managing people, resources and projects and programmes. They are full of sound practical advice about good practice. In Chapter 4 we take you through all the stages and tasks associated with managing people from recruiting staff, through supervision and teamwork, to how to manage their performance and where necessary undertake disciplinary processes. It emphasises very strongly how crucial it is to manage staff well as they are the key resource of our people profession. It also attends to values by emphasising good inclusive practice in the way you treat and support your staff to enable them to be effective youth workers.

In Chapter 5 we include management of all the other resources beyond the staff. We concentrate substantially on managing money, for which most professional youth workers have responsibility and for which many feel a level of understandable anxiety. We explore accountability, probity and delegation, and provide plenty of practical detail about planning budgets and monitoring spending. Health and safety is also everyone's responsibility and is integral to all our work. Your critical role in this is emphasised. Many youth workers are responsible for buildings so we discuss this too. Finally there is a list of detailed reminders about the management of other resources such as insurance.

Contemporary youth work very often includes short-term projects and programmes. Chapter 6 discusses thoroughly the management of these, working through many of the requisite skills of bidding for the funds; putting necessary systems and procedures in place; planning over the project's time span; and developing the project team. We also cover the ongoing work of project maintenance and problem solving. Whilst we know that most youth work needs to be evaluated, funded projects need considerable attention to monitoring and evaluating of specific outputs and outcomes. We provide structures, questions and suggestions to help you with this work. There is also a reminder about the need to publicise your work and recognise the influence you can have through sharing positive results.

Chapters 7 and 8 explore youth work's external environment and the changes that youth workers and their managers need to respond to. We start in Chapter 7 by recognising that government expects local public sector organisations to secure services, including positive activities for young people, by commissioning them rather than necessarily providing them directly. We look at procurement and other aspects of commissioning in detail to help you understand what this means for youth work and your role as provider or commissioner/purchaser. The chapter returns to the topic of performance management, this time in relation to targets and organisational effectiveness. We also examine relevant skills for working with others such as understanding stakeholders, working in partnerships and networking. We remind you again how important it is for youth work to continue to do what it does well – innovate – and to do more of what it has not always done so well – broadcast the value of our work.

Chapter 8 returns to the value of recognising 'the big picture'. We provide an overview of key policy messages which influence how youth work is currently delivered in England and which are intended to ensure it is meeting local need effectively. These include actively involving young people as young citizens and service users and devolving decisions and services as locally as possible and in a joined-up manner. We argue that you need to develop your own perspective on all this and be able to manage its complexity especially with respect to your engagement of young people and communities in influencing services. We emphasise the importance of extending your influence, a regular message in the book.

At the time of publication little has been published specifically for youth work about management aimed particularly at the professional worker and local manager. We have drawn upon our experiences as evaluators, inspectors, consultants and researchers of youth work, as managers of services for young people, and as teachers of people training to be professional youth workers and trainers of youth work managers undertaking management development. The next few chapters provide information and analysis and lots of sound practical advice which we hope will help you with your complex, challenging and exciting management work.

FURTHER READING

Deer Richardson, L and Wolfe, M (2001) *Principles and practice of informal education.* London: Routledge.

Grey, C (2009) *A very short, fairly interesting and reasonably cheap book about studying organisations.* 2nd edition. London: Sage.

Harrison, R, Benjamin, C, Curran, S and Hunter, R (eds) (2007) *Leading work with young people.* London: Sage.

Haynes, P (2003) *Managing complexity in the public services.* Berkshire: Open University Press. See Chapter 1 for a very helpful discussion about responsibility to politicians and citizens.

Ingram, I and Harris, J (2001) *Delivering good youth work.* Dorset: Russell House.

Sapin, K (2009) *Essential skills for youth work practice.* London: Sage.

Watson, TJ (2006) *Organising and managing work,* 2nd edition. Harlow: Financial Times/ Prentice Hall.

USEFUL WEBSITES

Lifelong Learning (**www.lluk.org.uk**).

REFERENCES

LLUK (2008 Appendix 2).

JNC (2007) Joint Negotiating Committee for Youth and Community Workers guidance on allocation to ranges. Appendix 1: 1–2, Appendix 2:1, Appendix 2:2.

Adirondack, S (2006) *Just about managing? Effective management for voluntary organisations and community groups.* London: London Voluntary Service Council.

Batsleer, J (2008) *Informal learning in youth work.* London; Sage.

Coulshed, V and Mullender, A (2006) *Management in social work,* 3rd edition. Hampshire: Palgrave Macmillan.

Davies, B and Merton, B (2009) *Squaring the circle.* Online: **http://dmu.ac.uk/Images/Squaring%20the%20Circle_tcm6-50166.pdf**

Department for Education and Skills (2003) *Every child matters.* London: DfES.

Department for Education and Skills (2005) *Youth matters.* London: DfES.

Department for Children, Schools and Families (2007) *Aiming high for young people: a ten-year strategy for positive activities.* London: DCSF.

Grey, C (2009) *A very short, fairly interesting and reasonably cheap book about studying organisations.* 2nd edition. London: Sage.

Haynes, P (2003) *Managing complexity in the public services.* Berkshire: Open University Press.

Mullins, L (2007) *Management and organisational behaviour,* 8th edition. Harlow: Financial Times/Prentice Hall.

OFSTED (2009) *Engaging young people: local authority youth work 2005–8.* Ref 080141.

Pollitt, C (2003) *The essential public manager.* Maidenhead: Open University Press.

Quinn, R (1988) *Beyond rational management.* San Francisco: Jossey-Bass.

Quinn, R, Faerman, S, Thompson, M, McGrath, M and St Clair, L (2007) *Becoming a master manager: a competency framework,* 4th edition. New York: Wiley.

Smith, MK (2002) 'Mary Parker Follett and informal education', *The encyclopedia of informal education.* Online: **www.infed.org/thinkers/et-foll.htm**

Watson, TJ (2001) *In search of management. Culture, chaos and control in managerial work,* 2nd edition. London: Thomson Learning.

Watson, TJ (2006). *Organising and managing work,* 2nd edition. Harlow: Financial Times/Prentice Hall.

Chapter 2

Managing yourself and your work

Mary Tyler

Achieving your Youth and Community Work degree

This chapter is about self-development in the context of management responsibilities and will help you to meet the following National Occupational Standards (February 2008).

- *5.1.1 Work as an effective and reflective practitioner*
- *5.1.2 Manage your own resources and professional development*
- *3.3.1 Develop productive working relationships with colleagues*

Introduction

Taking on responsibility as a professional worker or manager is exciting but it can also be pretty daunting. In this book's introduction, the concept of the youth worker at the hub of the wheel was presented. We continue with a vehicle analogy looking at how you control and steer, starting with yourself, your driving habits, how you choose your route for your journey and your signalling to others as you drive. This chapter considers how to manage yourself and your own work by looking at how you maintain control of both. It stresses the importance of your values as a guide to your work and its priorities. Advice is offered on time management and how you need to present yourself and communicate with colleagues in and beyond your organisation.

Being in control

ACTIVITY **2.1**

Think about yourself at the centre of a number of concentric circles with family and friends you are close to in the circle next to you and as you move outwards then perhaps young people, colleagues and managers. This would be followed in the next circle by community members, local politicians and any members of your board. Further out will be

---

national government, which for some will be at two levels, then the European Union and finally global organisations and influences (such as the United Nations, Microsoft, Shell and the World Bank) at the outer edge.

This activity could be a valuable one to do with a colleague.

- *Which of these circles and their members are you aware of on a day-to-day basis? Sketch them out if you wish.*

- *What kinds of influences do these people and organisations have on you and your work? Which can you have some control over and how?*

This activity may have reminded you of the complex world that surrounds you. We have to learn to live with this complexity and use what influence we have as managers of youth work (this is discussed further in Chapter 8). Clearly you have little control over much of this complexity, especially as an individual. You cannot undo family history and it can be extremely difficult to prevent a war. You cannot ensure you will not be run over by a bus; however, you can take care to cross the road carefully. You cannot ensure your staff meeting will be successful but you can shape it to some extent by preparing well, for instance, identifying decisions that need to be made, listing everyone's agenda items and ensuring everyone has all the information they need well in advance. You cannot prevent some things that arrive out of the blue, such as the aggressive and drunken parent who arrives at your project during activities, but you can try to minimise their impact by having plans and strategies in place to deal with them without chaos or panic. These examples involve you taking some control but you can only do so much where other people are also involved. You can take more control when the results are very largely dependent on yourself.

Being in control of yourself and your work is crucial to managing youth work. If you are not in control of yourself, then certainly nobody else will be. If you are not in control of your own behaviour, you will not be doing good youth work as you will not, for instance, be reliable in turning up, you will not know what you are going to do in a session, or you will not be consistent enough to provide young people with boundaries, some security and trust. Problems could escalate into a vicious circle. If you are not in control of yourself, then you cannot expect other staff and the project's young people to be in control.

Identify a couple of experienced workers/managers who seem to be in control.

- *How do you know this?*

- *What do they do?*

- *What do they not do?*

- *What do they say?*

Whilst being in control means something a little different for each person, confidence, competence and clarity are some key interlinked features. Clarity involves you having a realistic assessment of what is well within your realm of control, what is partly within your control and what is largely not within your control. This enables you to concentrate on what you can do rather than what you cannot. Being in control also means you know and understand the responsibilities you carry and the tasks you have to achieve and have a realistic plan about how and when you are going to do them. Additionally, you communicate your plan to those who need to know, and you are assertive and say no to additional work, but are open to negotiating changes in priorities.

If you are in control, you give yourself and others confidence. Being in control arises from providing clarity in many different ways to the young people you work with. For instance, they know what is happening at a session, what kind of behaviour is expected and what is not acceptable, and that you will listen and deal with issues fairly but firmly. This will provide an overall sense of purpose and confidence and should create a virtuous circle of positive experiences as young people see and experience a well-managed and therefore safe environment. Some of the young people you are working with will need this as a contrast to much of their everyday experience, especially of life outside school. Some will also soon find ways to undermine you if you are not in control.

Being in control reduces stress. A level of stress can be helpful in ensuring we are stimulated to work at our best, but too much can make us ill and knock our confidence too and it can take time to recover.

Recognise the impact of not being in control. You may think that you do not need to worry about planning ahead much because you work well under pressure. However, what is the source of this pressure? What if it is mainly self-induced because you leave tasks till the last minute that could have been done earlier and then, for instance, you are ill and cannot complete it, or the essential equipment has been booked earlier by someone else? Who suffers? Who may get stressed? Why do others always have to chase you for things? Who is unhappy if this keeps happening and how do they come to view you?

Being in control helps to ensure the quality of your youth work because it means that you have been reflecting on and planning your work. One of youth work's strengths is being able to work spontaneously with young people's interests and concerns by responding through conversation and with creative experiences and learning opportunities. This is based on having a very clear set of values, strong sense of purpose and a commitment to the centrality of the relationship process in which you are the key human tool. It is also based on being well informed, always applying good observation and listening skills and plenty of well-honed questions and activities from 'up your sleeve'.

There are a number of ways to improve your ability to be in control. First, to *be* in control you need to *feel* in control. Feeling in control is about knowing that you are competent, that you have sufficient training, information and support and that you have the time you need to achieve your tasks successfully. It is about planning – knowing what you want to achieve and how you will achieve it.

If you are not feeling in control, do something about it. Try to work out what is causing this feeling. If the cause is beyond your work in other aspects of your life, consider whether, once you have recognised this, you can 'box it up' and 'put it on a shelf' whilst you deal with the day's demands. If not, do you need to share it with your manager so they may be more sensitive about your workload for a while? If you have a particular task that is worrying you or feels too big, then talk about it with someone who can act as a listening ear or has relevant experience or skills to offer. Make a start with the task by identifying its constituent parts with the intention of taking little steps towards it. Avoid having unrealistic expectations such as 'I'll get all this done today'. If, for example, you have an evaluation report to write, start gathering the figures and case studies you need for it. Work out what headings you think it needs and start jotting down ideas for the content. You may find that once you make a start, the task begins to feel more manageable so that, whilst it may still need considerable time, you feel in control of it.

Second, you need to *know yourself and your behaviour patterns*. For instance, what upsets you; how excitement affects you; what impact your personal and work history may have had on you with respect to organising yourself; what time of day is best for thinking through ideas and tasks and getting them written down; and what time of day you benefit most from a break.

Very often in youth work you will not be working a standard nine to five day, so that can make it harder, but you have to plan to ensure that your work, and that of others, gets done. There will be fixed points that you can build some of your working hours round, such as the weekly team planning session or your monthly supervision session with your manager. Avoid going into your office an hour earlier to catch up on your emails before the meeting if you know that you will end up using it all to catch up on the gossip when you could do that more briefly after the meeting. Do your emails elsewhere or at another point in the day when you can be without distractions. The danger, when there is a flexible day, is that you end up working more hours than you are paid for with the result that you may well be too tired to do your key youth work and its management well. The staff you manage who need advice and support require you to be fresh enough to be able to help them think through their work.

Try to get the best balance for your own situation. So if you really cannot avoid an occasional day that starts with a 10 a.m. meeting and finishes with a post-session evaluation at 9.45 p.m., at least try to organise a visit home for a substantial afternoon break or share a sandwich with a colleague away from your desk. If you can spot a day like that coming up, think about how that has happened and why and, if you could have anticipated it, why you have let that day develop. Could you have improved your diary planning? Was it the best way to handle that week's demands? If there is no avoiding it, at least make sure you have planned the next working day to start later or to be a short one to catch up with yourself.

Third, try *not to let past patterns rule you*. Just because you have a tendency to be late for everything does not mean you cannot arrive on time. Leave for work earlier. If you find you often have unused holiday leave and you lose some every year, then start marking out your time off in your diary at or before the beginning of the leave year. If your view is that this is all too difficult, that you cannot change, then reflect on what you expect of the young people you work with.

Perhaps you have a wonderful ability to strike up conversations and build rapport quickly with young people and you are very imaginative in using arts and music in your work.

However, you hide behind your dyslexia as an excuse for not keeping stocked up with arts materials or getting round to writing up some examples of the good work you have been doing to help with promoting youth work. Maybe you have been the largely silent member of your team meeting with your school-based colleagues who have become so used to this that you are being drawn into strategies you are uneasy about when you could have contributed your own valid and possibly more appropriate ideas. Perhaps your new part-time detached workers are following you around letting you take the initiative in talking to unfamiliar young people, which you love doing. However, you need to be moving on, you need to be starting other projects which are queuing up. Your role now is about supporting their development of their street work skills, so you need to step back. Identify your negative patterns and their effect on your work and start changing them. They should not be allowed to limit you.

We will return to this topic in Chapter 8 when we consider taking responsibility and developing your influence after looking in some depth at the national and community levels of the circles introduced in Activity 2.1 at the beginning of this chapter.

Prioritising and values

In order to understand your tasks as a manager, a professional and therefore as a critical thinker, as already mentioned in Chapter 1, you need to *understand the bigger picture* within which our work is placed. While you are responsible for pieces of the jigsaw, you need to have the picture on its box in your head so you can locate your pieces. What part will this task play in enabling you to deliver a good youth work service? How does this youth work meet our funders' targets? Where does this work fit in terms of government intention and policy? How comfortable are you with these intentions?

Returning to the vehicle analogy used at the start of the chapter, the worker is the driver in control of the vehicle who needs to know and understand the purpose of the journey on which they are taking themselves and their passengers. The possible routes and what might influence your choice are another consideration. This assumes that you as this worker know why you have chosen to be a youth worker in the first place. Your motivation for youth work will be informed by your values and beliefs about society and young people and about work that is worthwhile as well as enjoyable and challenging (Banks, 1999). These values will have been shaped and clarified as you have developed as a critical and reflective practitioner increasingly committed to anti-oppressive work (Thompson, 2006). These values need to remain at the forefront of your mind as a mental satnav when you are focusing on managing, influencing the way you drive as well as your chosen route. You can easily lose sight of them, especially when the pressure is on to be delivering and presenting results, rather than reflecting on and questioning what you are doing and with whom.

With a good understanding of the work and clarity about your values and principles, you can then better shape your priorities, ensuring your work is congruent with your values. Job satisfaction arises from achieving the *most important tasks*. Which are the most important? Who has the power to decide? Whose agendas are you prioritising – young people's or adults' agendas?

ACTIVITY **2.3**

Take a significant youth work or management task you will be undertaking in the next week. Consider why you are doing it, who expects you to do it, who will benefit and who will be interested in what outcomes you achieve.

Benefits and outcomes are explored in more detail in Chapter 7. Equipped with a strong motivation for being in control and some ideas for how to achieve this, you need now to set your priorities and manage your time in order to meet them.

Managing time

It is important to realise the value of the key time management life skills that you have already as you have managed your time across employment, relationships and family, and leisure and study. These skills need developing as they are also very important in helping to manage your increasingly complex responsibilities in youth work.

A call centre worker has little choice about what they do. The youth worker in contrast has a relatively high degree of freedom about how to spend their work time, what meetings they choose to attend, what activities they do with young people and even what times they work as long as the work achieves its purpose. At one extreme is the worker who works all hours with young people, never takes their leave and is always late with administration; at the other is someone who counts every minute for 'time off in lieu' and always has a reason why something cannot be done.

As discussed above, if you do not take control of your time, this can lead to chaos and can mean young people will suffer. There is no shortage of time-management gurus and courses to attend if you need help and helpful techniques are available (try www.business-balls.com and O'Connell, 2008). There are, however, a few simple principles and you may be able to add more from your own experience.

- Keep your diary meticulously. Check it at least once a day and look well ahead weekly. 'Outlook' and other such systems can remind you electronically but remember to look further ahead too at what's coming up.

- Put in deadlines (such as the deadline for returning the monitoring form for your project's Lottery grant). Work backwards from those deadlines to plan the steps necessary to achieve the work on time.

- Try to add another 25 per cent to your first estimate of the time a task will take – most of us underestimate.

- Keep a list of jobs to be done (and make sure they are done and ticked off).

- Prioritise these jobs using your understanding of what is most important as well as what is most urgent.

- Organise yourself (for example, your filing or lists of contact details for key people).

- Plan in specific times each day to check your emails and do your administrative tasks and don't let them take over.

- Learn to delegate appropriately.

- Learn to say 'no'.

- Try to concentrate on one thing at a time and get it done (easier said than done, of course, but still worth a try). This could mean not being available to staff whilst you ensure you complete a demanding task (such as writing a finding bid that will keep them in a job).

- Take an overall look at how you are spending your time. What is the proportion of 'face-to-face' work with young people, supervision of staff, meetings, administration and so on? Is it about right? If not, you may be overloaded or escaping from part of the job you do not like or confused about what you should be doing. You may need to talk it over with your manager (see 'Managing your manager' below).

- Take time off and holidays. Dedicated workers are little use when they are 'burned out'.

- Be prepared to account for your time, in whatever way your organisation requires. You receive a salary and it is not unreasonable to be expected to be able to show how much time you worked and how you spent it.

Charles Handy says that *the manager is, above all, responsible for the future* (Handy, 1999, p331). The manager needs to look ahead, to plan, to develop staff, to anticipate problems, to bring in resources. Handy argues that the more senior the manager becomes, the longer their 'time-horizon' should be and the more time they should be spending thinking about future issues (working strategically). As a project worker you may have an excellent drama session arranged for tonight but to achieve a successful residential in six months time, your planning also needs to start now. As a senior youth officer you may be concerned about today's staff meeting but you also need to be asking whether these workers will be able to cope with the potential of changing technology in five years' time. The good manager lives in more than one time dimension dealing with 'now' but planning creatively for the future and avoiding the build up of crises.

Communication and presentation

Whilst the balance of responsibilities will vary depending on where you are located in your organisation and in its hierarchy, all youth workers/managers need to spend a great deal of time working with colleagues. This means you need to think about how you communicate in a range of contexts. This could include how you present yourself as the representative of youth work at multi-agency meetings or how you best provide support for a new volunteer after a demanding project session.

Youth work skills in relationship building and good communication with young people are entirely relevant to management communication. Effective communication in both cases relies on a good level of emotional intelligence. Daniel Goleman (1999) presents this as the ability to recognise our own feelings and the feelings of those around us and to use this to help us to manage situations and relationships. You need to be developing and using your self-awareness and ability to empathise as a manager in youth work. Key to good communication is how you present yourself.

The youth work field throws up unusual questions about how you manage the presentation of yourself to others. Youth workers are not 'suits' working in an office environment and they may move between very different contexts in the course of a working day, often forming a bridge between young people and adults. Youth workers do not generally have a uniform (like a nurse or a police constable) to inform the world about their role, although they would normally wear visible identification if they work on the street. They may even have choices about what to tell young people about who they are and why they are there.

Goffman's classic study of the presentation of self (Goffman, 1959) shows us how people handle their different roles and identities, embracing them, denying them or distancing themselves from them. Individuals are constantly choosing how to present their identity or the image of their 'team'. This is crucial for young people who will often be trying to look good in front of their mates and to avoid humiliation by adults in authority. Majors, for instance, describes how 'cool pose' is critical for many African–American young men giving them some control in a world where they have access to few resources, helping them look competent and perform with flair to different audiences – aiding survival but sometimes distancing them from help (Majors and Billson, 1992). Managers also choose how to perform their roles, their style and how they communicate. The best are leaders who know themselves and can help others to trust them.

The key to this difficult area of self-presentation is to think about how you appear to other people and how they may interpret what you do. Speech, body language and dress create their own expectations and assumptions about your role and competence. Other issues, such as friendliness, punctuality, reliability, commitment to the task, positive attitudes to other people and maybe prior information about you all affect how young people and adult colleagues see you. Inappropriate presentation in one context can wreck the good work you have done in another.

This is not to say that youth workers should become actors, endlessly playing a part that is not really true to themselves. This is one way to deal with the question of presentation but it is a dangerous route. It tends to conflict with the straightforwardness that builds trust and young people especially sniff out dishonesty with ease (not least because they often have to act themselves). You need to be yourself in this management role. There is usually plenty of scope for flexibility and adjustment to context and role without sacrificing your own integrity. In the last resort, if you feel your integrity is fundamentally compromised by what you are required to do and the issues cannot be resolved, you have the archetypal right of every worker to 'withdraw their labour' – you can resign.

Respect

Mark works on a drugs prevention project. His job involves working with young people who have been referred to the project for support because they use drugs or are at risk of involvement; information sessions for schools; and liaison with other agencies involved in combating drug misuse such as the police and health services.

Mark often works evenings and 'out of hours' to support young people. He always dresses casually, has dreadlocks and his style seems to add to his approachability. He has an extensive knowledge of the local drug cultures and has no problem understanding the street terms that the young people use.

Mark never changes how he dresses to go into schools or go to meetings. He plans his diary carefully so that he attends meetings on time. He will have read the agenda and never has his mobile on in a meeting. He always sends apologies on the rare occasions when a severe crisis with a young person prevents attendance and makes sure school sessions are always covered by one of his team if he really cannot make it. He allows enough time nearly every day to respond to messages and emails.

Mark is well respected by colleagues from other agencies. They feel his understanding of youth culture is a real asset and he does not take up time complaining about the difficulties of his job. He writes good reports and several of his recommendations have been taken up by the Drugs Action Team.

ACTIVITY **2.4**

- *What factors do you think are helping Mark to gain respect?*

- *Are there any you might want to apply?*

- *What kinds of assumptions could be made, for instance, by a headteacher or a health service manager, about 'typical' youth workers they perceive as presenting themselves badly?*

Youth workers inevitably influence colleagues and those they manage as role models in the way they conduct themselves and the way they work with young people. You need to recognise this form of communication/presentation, use it to the advantage of good youth work and be as effective a role model as possible. You need credibility and respect and to be seen as authoritative with a positive approach to your work. So as a manager you need to be self-aware, conscious of how others perceive you and open to further self-development in the same way as you should be in your role as a youth worker with young people.

Listening is often going to be more important than speaking. By listening (and observing) you will find out what is going on, going well and not so well. You will be able to then reflect on what you hear and make decisions about where to intervene and where to leave well alone. Kolb's reflective learning cycle is relevant here (in, for instance, Doherty, 2002, p416; Hawkins and Shohet, 2007, p19). By listening actively you may better enable that part-time worker to work through to some solutions in their work with a young person, learning as they go, rather than simply by telling them what to do. Often it is about asking appropriate questions. Try to ask what, why and how questions to develop understanding – yours and other people's.

Providing positive feedback and recognition is also important. Look for opportunities to tell colleagues and those you manage that they are doing well, whether it be the delivery of a whole programme at the final evaluation or that they handled a brewing conflict in a group session. This can provide increased confidence which not only improves a worker's wellbeing but can also lead to better work as confident staff will generally be more effective in their work with young people and may be more inclined to try new approaches.

Body language says a great deal, so be aware of this too. When you are with staff you manage, make sure you give them the feeling that you are alongside physically and mentally, sit down together, give them all your attention, turn off your mobile and use eye contact (unless this is culturally inappropriate). Only when you have spent that time together do you then move on to the next task.

Communication in organisations

Often as a professional youth worker your role as a manager of youth work is in the middle of the organisation – working with both front-line youth workers and senior managers. You have to be both a buffer and a channel of communication. This can be difficult, especially when some of what you are doing is managing change. There is always a need to communicate even if it is simply to say that you are not sure what is happening about the restructuring and explaining that the delay is due, for instance, to the need for the board or key councillors yet to decide which strategy is to be pursued. Too often staff complain that they are told nothing and feel like the proverbial mushrooms in the dark. Better they understand that decisions that will affect them are complex and that you also have limited information, and to acknowledge the worries and concerns and to explore them together but then move on to matters that you can control.

As the buffer you may need to deal with the demands of the organisation by, for instance, translating and representing the work on your project to those above in target terms rather than simply transferring those demands for targets directly to those employed to deliver. In this way you leave the front-line workers to focus on what they are best at. You need to be an advocate for your project's work as discussed further in Chapter 4. You do, however, also need to ensure workers understand the importance of recording and evidencing their work to increase its credibility with those they may themselves not be in contact with. You can encourage a creative approach, telling stories about good youth work.

You can use meetings as effective communication opportunities, especially those that you are responsible for. It can be easy for meetings to fall into a set pattern but they can be designed to enable good two-way communication as you and your staff can develop a shared understanding of the latest expectations of you by your organisation, review, plan and share dilemmas and good practice. Take care to use this expensive and precious time resource well (Adirondack, 2006). Maybe you could encourage ownership by members by, for instance, taking turns at chairing and minuting, and identifying some items together for the next meeting.

There are several types of commonly recognised management styles, some of which are more congruent than others with youth work as they reflect commitment to respect and anti-oppressive practice in the way you manage. What are your perceptions of your colleagues? Do you see them as largely committed to doing a good job for and with young people and therefore people who will flourish in work when given the space and flexibility to do so? Unfortunately the impact of the business culture and targets (more on this in Chapter 7) can lead to youth work managers becoming very outcome-focused and they may need to be reminded to value the steady and educational process of youth work undertaken by their staff. At different times teams need you to manage them in different ways or at different places on a continuum between tight control and direction and a laissez-faire approach. This depends on, for instance, how new the team members are and how long the team has been in existence as well as the personal situation of each individual and their skills and aspirations (styles are discussed further in Chapter 4).

Some aspects of communication can be achieved via email when necessary. This method is certainly ideal for supplying information and making arrangements, particularly across large numbers of people in an organisation. It will never be suitable for any support or developmental tasks with colleagues or staff you manage that rely on meaningful working relationships. Nor is it useful for dealing with issues.

Some issues cannot be resolved by you as the worker alone without action or understanding on the part of your manager. Suppose that Mark from the earlier example cannot complete all the school drug education sessions to meet his targets because the numbers of young people directly referred to the project for drug misuse is rising sharply. How would he be best placed to resolve the problem? Faced with stress from a lack of support, pressures of overload, or conflicts between your various roles and targets you, like Mark, may need to talk to your line-manager or perhaps your board. They need to understand the changing circumstances. Remember you are the expert on the situation as the person at the front line.

Good management of your work involves managing the relationships above you as well as those below you. Again this is all about communication. It pays off to discuss your job description, explain where the tensions lie and try to agree priorities. Ask clearly for the support and resources you need and make sure you get regular supervision and use these sessions effectively. Keep your manager informed, alert them early if there are problems brewing and if necessary put your concerns in writing. Remember that your manager will want to avoid complaints and crises and will have their own targets to meet – helpfulness and insight on your part will go a long way.

You may have an advisory committee or a board of directors. In the voluntary sector, this is especially important constitutionally (see 'Setting up infrastructures' in Chapter 6). You need to put in effort to make sure the committee works for you – regard them as a positive asset. To be able to support you effectively, members of a committee or board need enough information about what you do and clear roles for themselves (Adirondack, 2006, pp18–20). Provide training, background documentation, visits to the project in action and, above all, offer genuine respect for their experience. You need a good relationship and communication with the Chair in particular. Constant moaning does not help but they do need to understand your difficulties as well as the successes. If you face dilemmas or need support, put the issues plainly and ask the committee to help in resolving these and setting priorities. You may be surprised how much a fully functioning committee can assist your work. Communicating with and managing your manager or board is discussed further in Chapter 8.

C H A P T E R   R E V I E W

This chapter focuses on the task of managing yourself and your work, the essential prerequisite for management of youth work. It emphasises:

- the importance of taking control, ways to achieve that and to feel more in control too;

- understanding the bigger picture so you know where your work fits, what role it plays;

- using your values which motivate you to also guide your understanding of and prioritising of tasks and applying plenty of time management strategies;

- presenting yourself and therefore youth work well to others;

- communicating well in a variety of circumstances when taking management responsibility in your workplace which helps ensure good youth work is happening.

FURTHER READING

Adirondack, S (2006) *Just about managing? Effective management for voluntary organisations and community groups.* London: London Voluntary Service Council.

Banks, S (1999) *Ethical issues in youth work.* London: Routledge (new edition due March 2010).

USEFUL WEBSITES

Helpful techniques **www.businessballs.com**

REFERENCES

Adirondack, S (2006) *Just about managing? Effective management for voluntary organisations and community groups.* London: London Voluntary Service Council.

Banks, S (1999) *Ethical issues in youth work.* London: Routledge.

Doherty, T and Horne, T (2002) *Managing public services.* London: Routledge.

Goffman, E (1959) *The presentation of self in everyday life.* London: Penguin.

Goleman, D (1999) *Working with emotional intelligence.* London: Bloomsbury.

Handy, C (1999) *Understanding organisations.* London: Penguin Books.

Hawkins, P and Shohet, R (2007) *Supervision in the helping professions,* 3rd edition. Maidenhead: Open University Press.

Majors, R and Billson, J (1992) *Cool pose. The dilemmas of black manhood in America.* San Francisco: Jossey-Bass.

O'Connell, F (2008) *How to get more done.* Edinburgh: Pearson Education Limited.

Thompson, N (2006) *Anti-discriminatory practice,* 4th edition. Hampshire: Palgrave.

Chapter 3
Managing in organisations

Mary Tyler

Achieving your Youth and Community Work degree
This chapter is about understanding the organisational context of your work and its impact on you and your colleagues. It has some relevance to the following National Occupational Standard (February 2008).

- *3.3.2 Develop productive working relationships with colleagues and stakeholders*

Introduction

This chapter places you and your work in the context of organisational life and encourages you to be a critical thinker about your work surroundings. Using the vehicle analogy applied in Chapter 2, we consider your position in your vehicle (your work) and in the local traffic (your organisation) and provide some maps and satellite photographs to help this process. You are introduced to two key organisational concepts, structure and culture, and you apply them in order to help you understand better your own and other organisations. Additionally you will become familiar with the 7–S framework and the learning organisation concept. The chapter will help you analyse your organisation and contribute to improving how it works, therefore enhancing the quality of its youth work.

Thinking about organisation

When we are considering management of our own work (whether it includes managing others or not), we are considering it in a context, the context of an organisation or several organisations. This organisation will influence the effectiveness of our work and vice versa since they are interlinked. Therefore it is imperative that you understand the organisation you work for and to a lesser extent those organisations that you work with and are in partnership with. This understanding will inform many actions you take in relation to both your own work and the work of others with whom you liaise or others whose work you manage. This can best be done by building a collection of perspectives (or specs) and concepts with which to view your organisation which, between them, will provide a rounded and complex picture to inform your work and the decisions you make.

To develop your understanding of organisations and to illustrate this notion of perspectives, we will introduce some common organisational concepts such as structure, culture and learning organisations that these perspectives emphasise, and apply them to our settings. These concepts demonstrate how different perspectives have contributed to our theorising and can help you to be a critical thinker about management in the same way that you are a critical thinker about work with young people. Some of these concepts may well be ones you have taken for granted. The theoretical perspectives from which these concepts originated have become popular at different times but remain so influential in our thinking that we do not necessarily recognise them for what they are. We consider two such perspectives very briefly to illustrate this.

The scientific management or classical perspective developed from the work of FW Taylor early in the last century (see, for instance, Mullins, 2007; Doherty and Horne, 2002). He was concerned with detailed scientific design of the various tasks needed to make the organisation's product and close supervision of people trained to carry them out. Typical concepts and language associated with this perspective include hierarchy, job descriptions, line management, quality and performance indicators. This way of thinking emphasised efficiency and assumed it was possible to develop the principles and to find the right formula for successful work and organisations. It led, for instance, to the development of Henry Ford's first car assembly line in 1913 (Mullins, 2007) and other mechanised work which we see today, for instance, in the highly structured work style of call centres. This may have been efficient for producing a physical product, the design of which did not change much. However, such production principles were applied to the design of the then relatively new public sector organisations delivering services to people such as medical care and social services. People were batched and processed (James, 1994, p48) and the public bureaucracies that were established grew vastly bigger after the Second World War with the development of the welfare state. This has had both pros and cons. While this approach may have achieved important efficiency and consistency in public services, it also has led to procedural hassles, 'red tape', inflexibility and practice divorced from user need.

The open systems perspective (mentioned in Chapter 1) which was developed in the 1960s and 1970s, originally by biologists and later by engineers, emphasised how an organisation can be seen as similar to an organism reacting to its environment and that each part of the organism is interconnected so that change in one part influences another. Organisations were also likened to machines undertaking a set of activities with the inputs they receive from their wider environment, such as students or raw materials such as oil, and transforming them into outputs such as vocationally qualified graduates or petrol. The perspective argued for the importance of organisational strategy, the organisation knowing what it intends to achieve and how, which is regularly updated based on monitoring changes in its environment such as the health of the economy. It also emphasised language such as inputs, processes, outputs and outcomes (Doherty and Horne, 2002; Quinn et al., 2007), terms which are now familiar to us in youth work and are discussed further in Chapters 6 and 7.

This approach to explaining organisations and work has its benefits in helping us identify links between our work, our organisations and wider society, and connections between different parts of the organisation, but this is only part of the story. For instance, significantly for youth work and its value base, the open systems perspective and, equally, the scientific management perspective gave little explicit recognition to power or its poten-tially oppressive nature in the workplace. Consider, for instance, the impact of institutionalised racism in the police force as reported by the Macpherson inquiry (1999) into the tragic death of Stephen Lawrence, a Black teenager killed in a racist murder in south London. This racism affected not only the way Black people were dealt with by the police but also Black staff in the force.

The classical/scientific management, the open systems perspectives and other *positivist* (scientific) perspectives all see organisations as objects and they set out to find the best ways to organise the work based on some key assumptions about the importance of, for example, stability, developing staff, or maximising output. In practice there will generally be several alternatives which are suitable and often we may not set out to follow a clear path because humans are not as methodical and rational as some perspectives tend to assume. The contrasting *interpretivist* perspectives recognise that organisations are made of individuals and groups of people with all their complex motivations, emotions, interests groups, power and game playing and in that sense organisations are social constructs, constructed by those involved, rather than objects. Each person may have a view on ways forward based on their interpretation of the organisation from their position in it, their experience and values and, for instance, their gender or race. Each of these subjective views is valid. Such perspectives are interested in understanding organisations and the people in them per se and not necessarily with any agenda about improving their effi-ciency. For further reading on the major organisational perspectives see the end of this chapter.

Using both types of perspectives and the concepts they have generated can enable us to appreciate the complexity of organisations. A number of the later chapters will draw on some common organisation theories. It is important at this stage to understand their ori-gins in the positivist and, to a lesser extent, the interpretivist perspectives and so therefore to be aware of how we should use such theories with a critical awareness about their assumptions and intentions.

Structure

ACTIVITY **3.1**

Find an up-to-date organisation chart of your current or recent workplace showing the relationships between the different jobs and teams, or if you don't have one try to draw one up from what you know.

- *Why are people grouped in the way that they are and what is the rationale for the way you are line managed?*
- *Are there people who seem to belong in more than one place?*
- *What happens when you ask two or three different people why the structures are the way they are?*
- *How clear is the boundary between your organisation and others it works with?*

Undertaking this activity is likely to show you that both the positivist and the interpretivist perspectives explained above have played a part in your reflection and any answers to these questions. For instance, in some cases it is clear that people are grouped because together they provide a service to a particular group of people. More than one colleague will explain a structure in this way. Indeed, organisation charts are intended to demonstrate that formal structure. In other cases you may find that nobody is sure why people are grouped as they are, that the grouping may be described in varied ways and that all may have different stories about why the current structures are in place.

Commonly the explanations for the varied kinds of organisational structures where youth work can be found include:

- the history of the organisation, which may involve key individuals;

- its aims and values;

- the impact of government policy (for instance the development of integrated youth support services);

- its size;

- the geographical spread of the organisation's area of responsibility;

- the nature of the kinds of activities it offers.

Some hypothetical case studies of organisations follow. As you read them think about a) the ways each organisation's structure illustrates some of the above factors, and b) the ways in which day-to-day work practice and its line management can vary in these different structures. You could imagine asking some people within these structures the same questions you answered above about your own organisation.

CASE STUDY

Morrells Place

Morells Place is a small voluntary youth organisation in a racially and culturally diverse neighbourhood. It is run by a committee of local people and it employs two full-time youth workers and some part-time staff. There are several volunteers too who help run various daytime and evening activities for young people and other community groups. One of the full-time workers, who was the only employee until the committee recently gained new funding, takes all responsibility for the day-to-day finances. Both of them provide advice to the part-time staff who work with the young people. Responsibility is shared for popping out to the cash and carry for supplies, remembering to put the bins out on collection day and transporting some of the young people, for instance, to the city arts events. Most of the applications for funds are prepared by a couple of the committee members. Everyone in the organisation knows each other. The structure is simple, most people have several responsibilities and many roles overlap.

CASE STUDY

Grantshire Sexual Health Team

The Sexual Health Team (GSHT) in the small county of Grantshire comprises staff employed by various parts of the local authority and the Primary Care Trust (PCT) including nurses, doctors, teachers, youth workers, administrative and multi-media staff – a total of 33 people. There are two offices, one in a hospital in the county town and the other smaller one some distance away in a shop front in a small market town. Each office houses staff from a mix but not all the professional groups. Like all the other professional groups, the youth workers are office based, mainly in the market town, and are managed as a small team by a youth work manager who is part of the management team based in the hospital reporting to the coordinator of the GSHT. This person in turn is a member of a senior management team in the PCT. One youth worker is seconded for 50 per cent of their time to a project in the main seaside town which works with teenage parents and is run by a national voluntary organisation. This worker is managed for that 50 per cent by the manager of that project who reports to their regional executive. This structure is complex. Some staff rarely meet while others work in the same office but have limited shared work, and some plan and work together on a variety of project teams. Most staff are located and managed in teams with others who share the same professional training and outlook.

CASE STUDY

East Lorchester Integrated Youth Support Service

East Lorchester Borough has a new Integrated Children and Young People's Service. It has organised its services into four geographical localities like most other council services. In each locality there is an Integrated Youth Support Service (IYSS) made up of three or four full-time youth workers and the part-time staff they manage, a teenage pregnancy worker and also several Youth Offending Services staff, Drugs and Alcohol workers, Connexions Personal Advisers (PAs), an education welfare officer (EWO), a part-time Parenting Support worker and administrators. Each locality has an IYSS manager and two or more deputy managers with a variety of professional backgrounds. Staff are each line managed by one of these managers who may or may not share their professional background and training. Some of those managers have borough-wide responsibilities too for work such as youth engagement, youth work, support for young people not in education, employment or training, the teenage pregnancy strategy and drugs and alcohol work. The youth workers are mostly based individually or in pairs in youth projects and each one is a member of a borough-wide group too, such as PAYP. For this borough-wide work they report to another manager often based in another area. So in this case there is a complex matrix structure with staff reporting to locality line managers for some of their work and to other line managers for other aspects of their work, a structure developed specifically in response to Every Child Matters and more recent policy such as Youth Matters and Aiming High for Young People (see Chapter 8 for more information). History and chance may play a part in whether a particular worker is managed by a fellow professional or one from another profession.

The reasons for different structures are not always as rational or practical as you might assume. As you reflect on what you know about some of these factors, you are already theorising about organisations. Several of these explanations may be relevant and any can be legitimate if they present the organisation in the way members perceive them. Organisations are socially constructed realities that are as much in people's minds as they are represented in organisational charts. This theorising provides you with ways of explaining what happens in your organisation and this in turn influences the way you operate in it and make decisions.

Culture

You will know that each place you may have worked (whether in youth work or not) has a different feel about it and different ways of doing everyday things such as greeting each other at the start of a working session. This is the culture, the informal aspects of the organisation, the daily practice which reflects the organisation's otherwise largely invisible values or ethos.

Organisational culture has been described in many ways. Morgan (1989, p157) calls it the 'social glue' that holds everything together, some of which is apparent such as how we celebrate a colleague's birthday and some of which is more subtle such as how far we follow organisational procedures. Other images Morgan uses that help us think about the concept of organisational culture, and its complexity and significance, include an iceberg (Morgan, 1997, p169; Mullins, 2007, p30) and an umbrella. We only see the formal aspects of the organisation such as policies and buildings, the parts of an iceberg above the surface of the sea. Culture is based on a much larger and deeper reality of attitudes, behaviour and communications, much of which is below the surface. Culture as an image of an umbrella illustrates how it can also be seen as the overarching values and visions which can link people all working for the same organisation.

The culture is the aspect of workplaces which can be positive enough to retain you through difficult times, or negative enough to drive you away even if the work is what you are keen to do. Each youth work team or inter-disciplinary children and young person's team may have a different culture from its neighbouring one. The culture of a team of

---

ACTIVITY **3.2**

Think about your current or recent workplace again.

- *What aspects of this culture are largely under the water as in the iceberg image?*

- *Can you identify a common culture? Do you feel you share in it?*

- *Is your team's culture in conflict with those of other teams, and if so, in what ways and what kinds of difficulty does this create?*

- *What could you do about this as a manager in such circumstances?*

- *In what ways might an informal style of some youth work teams work in their favour or not alongside cultures of other teams influenced differently by their particular work style and organisational role such as health and safety or marketing and promotions?*

youth workers may be very different from a team of teachers or youth offending staff for example, even though they all work with the same young people in the same neighbourhood and/or in the same organisation.

You could find that the culture of the organisation you begin work in is more suited to the kind of small stable organisation it used to be. Perhaps long-standing youth work staff are resistant to regularly changing their working week which they are now expected to do as the organisation develops more frequently changing responsive projects. As a manager you play a part in creating, influencing and changing the culture simply through the impact of your style and personality and as a role model. If you set out purposely to influence the culture, you need to know where you are going, be open and ethical in your approach and be realistic about what you can achieve. Ideally you are aiming for more inclusive relationships and practice. It can be tricky to make change and it takes time but it can also be achieved in more significant ways such as reducing the length of a planned youth work session or staff meeting and expecting colleagues to drink a cup of tea together to conclude it while reflecting on how it went, removing the 'winner stays on' rule about the pool table in the youth project, or removing the table altogether and replacing it with comfy sofas.

Handy (1999) has developed Harrison's categories of culture into four types – power, role, task and person – which often prove useful in analysing the cultures you experience. Power cultures generally have a few powerful people at the centre who control much of what happens. This kind of culture is more common in small organisations with limited procedures in which individuals can have significant influence. In contrast a role culture depends substantially on people knowing their place and responsibilities and following the rules. Job descriptions are especially important and these and hierarchical position are key sources of power. In a task culture, emphasis is on achieving tasks by bringing suitably experienced people together in often-changing project groups – a 'get things done' culture. Power is associated with expertise. The person culture is probably the least common. This is a culture about individual autonomy where any organisational structure only exists because a group of workers will gain some mutual benefit. For example, a chamber of barristers need an organisation so that they can share administrative support, but each works independently and is not controlled by the other barristers. If you work in a large and diverse organisation, you may be able to identify all those cultures in different parts of the organisation.

CASE STUDY

Pratima's first meeting

Pratima has started in her first post at East Lorchester after qualifying as a youth worker. She goes to her first borough-wide youth work meeting with other local professional colleagues soon after settling in and getting to know some young people in the neighbourhood. Most people arrive literally as the meeting begins and some are late. The agenda is lengthy and much of it concerns targets, funding, inspection and the recent restructuring. Discussion is limited as much of the meeting is taken up with managers explaining aspects of these topics. People are friendly to their new colleague but mostly rush off as soon as the meeting finishes. Pratima leaves disappointed as she has had little opportunity to meet colleagues or learn about their work.

ACTIVITY *3.3*

- *If you were Pratima, how might you respond after the meeting?*

- *What might this experience say about Pratima's expectations, the culture of the organisation she has joined and the impact of the world beyond the organisation?*

Earlier in the chapter when explaining the open systems perspective, we likened the organisation to a machine and organism. Culture is another such metaphor (Morgan, 2006), another way of seeing organisations which emphasises the everyday and how this has meaning and power so that, for instance, regularly using language such as targets, performance management and outcomes influences our perception of the organisation's purpose. This machine-like and managerialist culture means that we are accustomed now to discussing our work as a question of meeting targets as much as we discuss it as working creatively, informally and educationally with young people.

Structure, culture and organisational analysis

At this stage, having considered structure and culture to help you develop your understanding of organisations, you may find it helpful to look at the McKinsey 7–S framework (Mullins, 2007, p758). This is a model developed in Peters and Waterman's study in the early 1980s which was attempting to identify the features of a number of companies successful at that time. Although the model, developed from the open systems perspective, has now been around sometime, it is still popular and useful. In fact it forms the basis of the National Youth Agency's Hear By Right standards framework for the active involvement of children and young people used across the statutory and voluntary sector (Badham and Wade, 2008). It indicates how seemingly relatively unrelated aspects of the organisation are interlinked and it emphasises how changes in any one of these aspects, as identified in Figure 3.1, can have effects on other aspects of the organisation. The top three Ss in the diagram are seen to be the 'harder' aspects and the lower three the 'softer' ones. The 'harder' aspects are more structural and can be more easily influenced by managers, while the 'softer' features are more cultural and are more resistant to change. Structural and cultural aspects influence each other and all are influenced by and influence any shared values.

This model can be used to take stock of your organisation in its current form. Consider whether the different aspects are consistent with each other, and reflect on what aspects need to change to achieve a different result. Try now, using aspects of this model, to undertake some organisational reflection and analysis. The two following activities use two case studies of the organisations presented earlier in the chapter to help you do so.

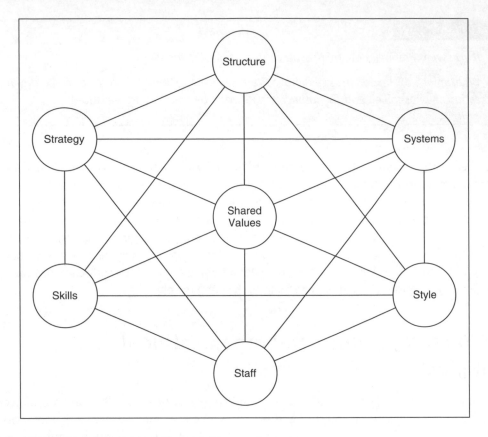

Figure 3.1 The McKinsey 7–S Framework

ACTIVITY 3.4

The Morrells Place case study

- *Does the structure appear to be a suitable one for its current purpose?*

- *What if the committee tender successfully to deliver all the youth work provision in their neighbourhood? This could mean that their budget and workload doubles and the project will need to collect far more monitoring data on their work. What might be the implications for their current systems? What kinds of changes might be needed?*

- *How would you describe the current culture at Morrells Place?*

- *In what ways, if any, might the culture change if the organisation grows as discussed?*

ACTIVITY 3.5

The Grantshire Sexual Health Team case study

- *In what ways might the skills of their immediate colleagues, their line management structure, or the style associated with the shop front or hospital office base lead to different organisational circumstances for different youth workers working for GSHT?*

- *What impact could some aspects of these circumstances have on the ability of youth workers to work to their particular strengths?*

Consider these and your earlier reflections on different organisation structures. Did each one seem to be the best structure for achieving that organisation's purposes? Do you think your own organisation has the right structure to achieve its purpose? Consider how one change in the organisation can lead to another. If your organisation gives all youth workers a Blackberry so they can communicate anywhere with one another by email and on all the social networks as well as phone and text, does everyone have the *skills* to manage this technology? How may this change contact making with young people? What impact could this have on holding boundaries between work and non-work life? Could such a change in *systems* and technology potentially have a detrimental effect on the *shared values* which concern not just overall expectations of enabling better lives for young people but also valuing the health of staff and not disturbing them in their personal time?

Maybe you and colleagues in your organisation, or teams within it, are encouraged to engage in substantial discussion and consultation about your work, its style and, for instance, how the organisation is structured. If so you are likely to be more open to change and improvements; indeed, you may make such decisions. In such circumstances a learning organisation develops.

The concept of a learning organisation, like the McKinsey's 7–S framework, was derived substantially from the open systems perspective. It is a concept that makes sense to youth work and its approach, that mirrors where you may wish your organisation to be, and that helps with understanding related popular management concepts such as quality and performance indicators.

A learning organisation is one which encourages its members to learn, and is regularly making changes to what it does and how it does it. It is an organisation which engages in what Argyris and Schon (1978, in Ranson and Stewart, 1994, p169) called double loop learning. Single loop learning involves considering whether the activities were carried out, whether they were done efficiently, and whether they had the planned effect – conventional evaluation (see Chapter 6 on how to do this well, and discussion about economy, efficiency and effectiveness and demonstrating value in Chapter 7). Double loop learning involves considering whether the activities *should* be carried out, whether different and new types of activities should be used instead and questions basic principles. A learning organisation treats this process of evaluation as a tin opening process rather than one about reading the dials (Everitt and Hardiker, 1996). Or to use our vehicle analogy again, the successful learning organisation is not just recording the miles, journey speeds and fuel consumption but is lifting the bonnet and examining the engine and, for instance, asking whether an engine designed to run on a more environmentally friendly fuel would be better for everyone. Both types of learning are needed. Single loop learning is part of maintaining the organisation, but in order for an organisation to survive in changing circumstances, it also needs to undertake double loop learning and engage in change.

ACTIVITY *3.6*

- *What kinds of single loop learning does your organisation engage you in?*

- *How much double loop learning happens?*

- *What kinds of key questions do you think your organisation would benefit from debating and why?*

- *How much do you involve young people in debate about the purpose of your organisation and how it is doing?*

Handy describes learning organisations as those 'which relish curiosity, questions and ideas, which allow space for experiment and reflection, which forgive mistakes and promote self-confidence' (1990, p199). They are those which value and use the expertise and experience of their staff to engage in improving the work and achievements of the organisation. Learning organisations are open to learning about their patterns, cultures and work in order to improve what they do and keep up with changes around them and impacting on them. In fact they are the kinds of organisations that are like ideal youth workers – open, responsive, inclusive, effective and reflective. You can see that this style of organisation is not only needed to survive in a competitive commercial world but also in the equally complex public and voluntary sector world of most youth work which is also increasingly competitive (see Chapter 7 on commissioning).

ACTIVITY *3.7*

Look back at the East Lorchester Integrated Youth Support Service case study and Activity 3.3 about Pratima's first borough-wide youth work meeting there.

- *What could Pratima do to influence the style of the meetings?*

- *If you were a senior youth work manager in East Lorchester what kinds of steps might you take to develop a learning culture in the IYSS?*

To keep focused on improvement, organisational members (key decision makers as well as front-line staff) need to be open to some fundamental questioning of what tends to be taken for granted. In the case of youth work this could be, for instance, debate about which groups your organisation works with in order that it can respond to those in most need as the population changes in an area where new migrants are settling. You may need to decide whether your work needs its own building bases or not and, if so, where they should be and what their purpose should be. You may even need to consider whether full-time youth workers will achieve more if they work mainly to recruit, train and support volunteers and reduce their face-to-face work with young people. This kind of double loop learning enables innovation, which should be a hallmark of good youth work (see Chapter 7 for detailed discussion on innovation).

Those who believe in learning organisations argue that they will be more successful because they engage in significant reflection and critiquing of what they do so they make important and appropriate changes to ensure they remain relevant. They are also better equipped to ensure their practice is anti-oppressive. So if you work in this kind of organisation, you will access learning opportunities and be debating with colleagues and young people about the purpose of some of your projects. You will also, for instance, be reviewing any change of focus driven by funding changes as opposed to the needs and concerns of the young people you know.

You can use the 7–S framework and the learning organisation concept to increase your understanding of both the structural (harder) and the cultural (softer) and how they are inextricably linked. Is the tail wagging the dog? For instance, does the management information system (MIS) demand a very particular approach to evaluating your youth work, such as identifying all the aspects of the curriculum you have covered in your youth work so they can be ticked for inputting on the system? In what ways does this approach and the way it has been introduced both help with and hinder your project from a focus on whether you are attracting and working successfully with sufficient young women or young disabled people for instance? Do you receive copies of the organisation wide per-formance data from the MIS that you input data into? Are you encouraged to use this system data to discuss with colleagues and help you with your planning or is it mainly seen as an input task to be done?

You can also use the 7–S framework and the learning organisation concept to help the organisation to adapt and respond to changes in the external environment. Chapters 7 and 8 explore youth work's external environment and the changes that youth workers and their managers need to respond to, while the chapters preceding it mainly help you with improving the management of the internal environment.

C H A P T E R   R E V I E W

This chapter has argued for the need for a critical understanding of your organisational setting. It has explored topics on:

- the benefit of using both positivist and interpretivist perspectives of organisations to develop a sufficiently complex picture;

- the need to be able to identify the structure of your organisation and the reasons for this structure as well as its suitability and impact on youth work;

- how to recognise the various cultures in your organisation displayed in different aspects of its work and in what ways you can influence them;

- using the McKinsey 7–S framework to take stock, and to understand the interplay between different facets of your organisation;

- applying both single and double loop learning, aspects of the concept of the learning organisation, to develop your own and your colleagues' evaluation of the way you all work and its suitability for your current circumstances.

FURTHER READING

Doherty, T and Horne, T (2002) *Managing public services.* London: Routledge.

Morgan, G (2006) *Images of organization*, 3rd edition. London: Sage.

Mullins, LJ (2007) *Management and organisational behaviour*, 8th edition. Harlow: Financial Times/Prentice Hall (or earlier editions).

REFERENCES

Argyris, C and Schon, D (1978) 'Organisational learning: a theory of action perspective', in Ranson, S and Stewart, J (eds) (1994) *Management for the public domain.* Oxford: Macmillan.

Badham, B and Wade, H (2008) *Hear by right.* Revised edition. Leicester: NYA.

Department for Education and Skills (2003) *Every child matters.* London: DfES.

Department for Education and Skills (2005) *Youth matters.* London: DfES.

Department for Children, Schools and Families (2007) *Aiming high for young people: a ten-year strategy for positive activities.* London: DCSF.

Doherty, T and Horne, T (2002) *Managing public services.* London: Routledge.

Everitt, A and Hardiker, P (1996) *Evaluating for good practice.* Basingstoke: Macmillan.

Handy, C (1990) *Understanding schools as organisations.* London: Penguin Books.

Handy, C (1993) *Understanding organisations,* 4th edition. Harmondsworth: Penguin Books.

Macpherson, W (1999) *The Stephen Lawrence Inquiry.* London: Stationery Office. Online: **www.archive.official-documents.co.uk/document/cm42/4262/4262.htm**

Morgan, G (1989) *Creative organization theory: a resource book.* London: Sage.

Morgan, G (1997) *Imaginization.* California: Sage.

Morgan, G (2006) *Images of organization*, 3rd edition. London: Sage.

Mullins, LJ (2007) *Management and organisational behaviour*, 8th edition. Harlow: Financial Times/Prentice Hall (or earlier editions).

Quinn, R, Faerman, S, Thompson, M, McGrath, M and St Clair, L (2007) *Becoming a master manager: a competency framework*, 4th edition. New York: Wiley.

Chapter 4
Managing people

Liz Hoggarth

Achieving your Youth and Community Work degree

This chapter is about leading and managing your staff both as teams and as individuals. It will help you to meet the following National Occupational Standards (February 2008).

- *5.2.1 Provide leadership for your team*

- *5.2.2 Allocate and check work in your team*

- *5.2.3 Recruit, select and keep colleagues*

- *5.3.1 Provide support to other workers*

Introduction

Youth work is often called one of the 'people professions'. We do not normally manufacture things or sell goods or services; we use the skills of adult staff to help and develop young people. It follows that if you are a manager in youth work, you will not only be dealing with people as your users but also dealing with people as your staff. In this chapter, we examine some of the key elements of good people management in this context, especially recruiting new staff and introducing them to the work, handling contracts, creating a climate of equality of opportunity in the workplace, supervision and appraisal, discipline and performance issues, and the meaning of support. We also discuss the concepts of leadership and teamwork that are so important and are therefore frequently echoed in other chapters.

Young people need to find a caring relationship with at least one adult they trust, within which they can learn, test things out and develop. Youth workers try to offer such relationships, often providing activities as a means to making good relationships and creating learning opportunities. There is ample evidence for the importance of trust in what makes effective work with young people (e.g. Merton et al., 2004, pp42–4; Hoggarth and Smith, 2004, pp190–1).

'Trust' involves such elements as reliability, honesty and safety. Creating a climate of trust is not just a matter of feelings (such as liking, caring or compassion), it requires real management skills. Young people cannot be expected to trust you or your organisation if, for instance, nobody can explain how the youth club funds are spent, or workers are constantly grumbling about how things are run or gossiping about the personal circumstances of the young people. We saw in Chapter 2 that whether you are a detached youth worker with no staff and no buildings to look after or a senior worker in a large project, you will need to manage yourself – how you use your time and how you present yourself to the young people and to other adults. Sooner or later you are likely to manage other people as well, whether that means part-time workers, volunteers or full-time staff and, as you will see in the next chapter, you may have to manage resources (money, buildings, equipment, materials). This chapter will help you to think through the principles of managing your staff and the practical issues involved.

Managing people

People are the most valuable resource of any organisation – without good people, projects fail. Your job as a manager is to draw out the best from that resource.

Most people thrive best in a job when they are clear about what they are supposed to be doing, they feel competent to do it and have some control over how it is done, they understand to whom they are accountable and they get some rewards for themselves from the work. Money is not the whole story; work also feeds a person's concept of themselves and if it constantly undermines that self-concept, they will become unhappy (Handy, 1999, pp51–9; Argyris, 1960). Effective managers try to find the best fit between the needs and motivations of their workers and the needs of the organisation, so that the energies and abilities of the staff are focused on the job that needs doing.

People management is a complex area. Employment law fills countless volumes; the law basically seeks to ensure fairness both to the employee and to the employer and to prevent unjust discrimination against individuals. The procedures are legion and there is an art to writing a good job description or the letter that invites someone to a disciplinary hearing. Do not try to cope by yourself. Take advice. Mistakes can be expensive and the goodwill of your staff is irreplaceable. If you work in a big organisation or a local authority, there will be a human resources department and you should take up relevant training and keep their guidance and any HR handbook available in your workplace. If you work in a tiny voluntary organisation, you can find companies that offer regular HR support for a fee or you can ensure that your board has plenty of people with the right skills to advise you. Some Councils of Voluntary Services (CVS) or other umbrella bodies also offer support and advice. Sandy Adirondack, whose writing we often refer to, provides a useful legal update section on her website www.sandy-a.co.uk. ACAS, the Advisory, Conciliation and Arbitration Service, offers free advice to individuals whether as employers or employees, together with training, resources and help with resolving conflicts at work. The ACAS website offers invaluable information on employment law and numerous specimen forms and advisory leaflets.

Recruitment

The process of managing people usually starts before you even meet them, whether you need a new worker or you are taking up a post with existing staff to manage. It is about the clarity of expectations and that issue of finding 'best fit'. The recruitment process needs to give the candidates enough detail about the post to make an informed choice and the employer the chance to be as certain as possible that they can do the job. Give care to the advertisement and the information pack as they will set the foundation for mutual understanding. A structure chart is useful and it is essential that a new member of staff is clear about their line of accountability. The job description and person specification are key tools for selection of staff. They inform the applicant – shortlisting and scoring or selecting at interview depend on them. Most organisations will have their own format but Adirondack offers good checklists of what they should contain (2006, pp81–3). You will need to decide how each element of the person specification will be assessed and whether any factors will be tested (for example typing or aptitude tests) or be a part of exercises such as a group discussion.

Interview days are important. Together with any information-giving sessions or tests, the interview gives the candidates an impression of the strengths and efficiency of your agency. You need to make sure that voluntary committee members and any other staff are fully briefed on the procedure. Young people are also more and more frequently involved in recruiting staff. They need to understand the process and be clear exactly how the final decision is made and their part in it. They need to take on board that the final choice may not be the candidate they prefer. Usually a list of questions is agreed that is put to every candidate, sometimes with follow-up questions allowed. Everybody needs to be clear about what they can and cannot ask, especially in areas that may be discriminatory. Everybody should take notes on each interview and these should be kept on file with a summary of the reasons for acceptance or rejection. It is a good rule of thumb to retain such notes for a period of at least six months afterwards in case of any complaints or legal claims (ACAS, 2005).

It is important to tell candidates the decision as soon as possible, including those who are not successful. It can be incredibly hurtful to hear second hand that someone else was appointed. Good candidates may go elsewhere if there are long delays. Whether the offer of appointment is made on the interview day or, as is more usual, by telephone later, it is essential that any conditions are made clear. Normally a reference will be requested and if the employee will work directly with young people, a Criminal Records Bureau check must be taken up. Some posts will also require medical checks.

It is against the law for any employer to appoint someone who is not entitled to work in the UK (Asylum and Immigration Act 1996). All applicants (not just those who appear to be from abroad or from a minority group) should be asked to produce the necessary documents and a copy should be kept. If an applicant is not entitled to work in this country, a work permit will be required.

Contract

All new employees who work for more than one month must be issued with a written statement of particulars of employment within the first two months of work (Employment Rights Act 1996). In practice it should be given as soon as possible and may be in the form of a letter of appointment. By law these principal 'particulars' must contain certain information, including the names of employer and employee, the job title and brief description, the date employment began, the date the employee began continuous employment, what they will be paid and when, hours of work, place of work, leave entitlement and holiday pay.

A contract of employment is also normally provided which includes not only the essential particulars but also all the terms and conditions of employment such as those relating to overtime, sickness, pensions, length of notice, disciplinary procedures, appeal and grievance. A job description is usually attached. The new employee is normally asked to sign the contract. It is not uncommon for organisations to fail to give the essential information to new workers. This is not only against the law but also sows the seeds of mistrust and confusion for the future.

Part-time staff

The youth work field has an unusually high proportion of part-time staff. After many years of tradition around informal appointments of so-called 'sessional staff', their rights are still often overlooked and their full potential is not developed.

The situation changed when Great Britain implemented European directives on part-time work, fixed-term work and working time (the Part-Time Workers [Prevention of Less Favourable Treatment] Regulations 2000 and Amendment 2002; Working Time Regulations 1998). This means that it is unlawful to treat part-timers less favourably than comparable full-time staff in respect of their terms and conditions, unless the difference can be objectively justified. In the youth work field this brought substantial changes in how part-timers were graded and their rights to paid leave.

All 'workers' are now entitled to a minimum of four weeks paid holiday or more if they are employed under JNC conditions or other more favourable terms. Annual leave is calculated on a *pro rata* basis for part-timers (that simply means their leave is proportionate to the hours they do).

Fixed-term posts

Fixed-term employment is becoming more and more common, particularly in view of the plethora of time-limited funding for work with children and young people. It is important to understand that fixed-term employees still have employment rights and should not be treated differently. In some circumstances they may become permanent. Fixed-term contracts cannot just be repeatedly renewed and in many situations they serve no useful purpose as the employee will accrue the main employment rights in any case. The main thresholds (IDS, 2001) are set out below. An employee:

- with *one* year's continuous service can claim unfair dismissal at the Employment Tribunal (see also 'Discipline' below) and for certain specific situations, such as dismissing a woman who is pregnant, no qualifying period applies;
- with *two* years' service is entitled to redundancy payment;

- with *four* years' continuous service is entitled to permanent status even if a contract has expired and a new one has been given (unless there have been real breaks in continuity or there are objective grounds for the fixed-term).

Casual workers

Youth work can also involve casual staff. It is important not to confuse this with part-time staffing. A casual worker is contracted for a short time for a specific task such as a summer play scheme or an arts project. Thirteen weeks is normally seen as the maximum length of a casual or temporary contract as beyond that workers start to accrue such rights as annual leave. If the short-term arrangements settle into a regular pattern, even if there are breaks, the individual may be able to argue that they have a contract of employment. Casual workers are often self-employed and advertisement may not be needed. If temporary staff are appointed to cover vacancies however, the post normally needs to be advertised and a part-time or full-time contract will usually follow for the appointed candidate.

The implications for the youth work manager of these categories of staff and the legislation that applies to them include the need to budget and plan for leave for part-timers, to calculate for the possibility of redundancy payments at the end of schemes with short-term funding and to exercise extreme care around casual and temporary positions. In all recruitment situations, it is crucial to avoid giving anybody the impression that they will automatically get the job in question, even if they have been working in your project on a part-time or temporary basis before. You may wish to encourage somebody to apply but recruitment should be a genuine process of opening up opportunity so that you can find the person best suited for the vacancy.

Volunteers and students

Youth work will often draw in volunteers, who are a real resource but can also be misused and fail to realise their full potential. Volunteers are essentially members of staff, they just do not get paid for their work. They deserve recognition, training, proper supervision and the same clarity about role and expectations that a paid staff member would receive. Best practice is to induct volunteers (including committee members) and give them a written description of their role in the organisation. They need to know if they are entitled to claim out-of-pocket expenses and how to do so. Volunteering England offers examples of 'volunteer agreements' which usefully spell out the obligations on both sides.

Students can be exploited too and are sometimes regarded as a free pair of extra hands. If you are thinking of taking on a student placement at your unit, you must be prepared to give proper attention to supervision, learning opportunities and liaison with the course tutors.

Equal opportunities in the workplace

In the world of youth work, we are trying to reach young people from a huge variety of backgrounds, many of whom face substantial challenges in their lives, and help them to cope and develop. To do that we need the most effective workers available, people who can bring their own insights to the work, develop their own skills and potential and provide role models for the young people. We need the widest pool of candidates possible and have strong imperatives for promoting equality of opportunity within our work places. Taking an interest in this topic, making good relationships with minority organisations in your own area and fostering positive attitudes amongst the whole team can pay enormous dividends for our service users. If your workplace is inclusive for staff, it is also likely to be inclusive for the young people it serves.

Regrettably, equality policies and legal frameworks are more often seen as unnecessary constraints, additional cost or as trivial issues of being politically correct. It is much easier to develop equality of opportunity in a positive way if you understand the guidance and regulations and the reasons behind them.

The law lays down that you cannot discriminate in employment on the grounds of someone's sex, gender reassignment, sexual orientation, status as a married person or civil partner, race, colour, age, nationality, ethnic origin, religion, beliefs or because of a disability, pregnancy, childbirth or subsequent maternity leave, or trade union membership. It is also unlawful to discriminate against part-time workers. You need to make 'reasonable adjustments' for a disabled person if they need them at interview or to do the job.

That is quite a list but it boils down to the same principle: it is about fairness in the workplace. Access to employment and development within it ought to be on the proverbial 'level playing field': the person with the most appropriate qualities and skills should get the job. Managers who treat their staff fairly and flexibly will be better able to recruit and retain good workers and harness their commitment. There are some rare situations where a 'genuine occupational requirement' may apply such as needing a woman to work with girls and young women on personal and sensitive sexual health issues, and if so, a post can be advertised citing the section of the relevant discrimination act. In general, you should consider carefully if this is really necessary and whether the person specification cannot be sufficiently precise to find the right person for the role. 'Positive action' is also within the law; it means taking steps to attract applicants or provide access to training where particular groups are historically underrepresented in the workforce. For example, if a service has no disabled workers or very few minority ethnic staff in an area with a large ethnic population, then advertisements may legitimately seek to attract such people but appointment will still depend on choosing the best candidate for the post.

Discrimination can be 'direct', that is, treating someone less favourably on one of the specific grounds above. It can also be indirect, which means applying an apparently general rule (such as requiring lengthy experience or certain forms of dress), which in practice disadvantages a particular group and cannot be justified in terms of the job to be done. 'Harassment' (that is, behaviour which is unwelcome or unacceptable and which results in a stressful or intimidating environment for the victim) and 'victimisation' (where somebody complains of discrimination in good faith and is then discriminated against because they did so) are also types of discrimination and are against the law. The need to avoid all these forms of discrimination applies to all aspects of dealing with staff including advertisement, recruitment and selection, interviewing, support and supervision, access to training and staff development. Your own agency will probably offer training on aspects of equalities or there are numerous courses promoted by other providers. The new Equality Bill currently being considered by parliament is intended to bring all the numerous aspects of equalities legislation together into one consistent and well-framed act, which should prove very helpful. You should take up such training especially if you will be involved in recruitment. There are numerous websites and government agencies that can assist you on particular questions (Business Link, 2007; ACAS, 2007; the Equality and Human Rights Commission).

ACTIVITY *4.1*

You have noticed that one of your female part-time workers, who is young and attractive, is being constantly bombarded with suggestive remarks, jokes and innuendo by the men on the team. She has not complained.

- *Do you regard this as something that is a natural part of youth work and feel that she will need to learn to cope with it or do you think it is something that requires some action on your part as a manager?*

- *If you think action is warranted, what would you do?*

Induction

New workers, full-time and part-time staff and volunteers, should all have a programme of induction. Its length will vary with the complexity of their role but will usually include a number of typical elements. When people arrive, the most urgent matters include those aspects that will help them to feel welcomed, comfortable and safe such as introductions to other staff, fire exits and procedures, tea/coffee facilities, settling in at the desk, email and telephone systems and basic supplies. It helps if new workers have some information to read about the agency or some simple tasks so that they are not stranded or bored. In the following weeks, the worker will need information on the structure of the agency and all the basic procedures appropriate to the post such as arrangements for time recording, leave or sickness; basic financial procedures such as placing an order or claiming expenses; computer access; team meetings; supervision, training and appraisal; trade unions. There may be essential training that the organisation requires such as minibus driving tests or health and safety courses.

The ideal is to have an induction programme drawn up for each new arrival. This will contain a list of what needs to be covered and show who is responsible for delivering each part. There should be a space to enter the date each item is completed and the whole programme makes a useful tool for early supervision sessions (there is a useful checklist in Adirondack, 2006, pp94–6). It is a natural part of valuing your staff to prepare for their arrival. Too many new workers suffer indignities such as having no proper work base or no computer links and such neglect can set up discontent for the future and will give a poor impression to other agencies.

Probation

Probationary periods are used by many employers, sometimes with draconian clauses that the employee can be dismissed without notice or appeal within the period. These have no specific meaning in law and an employee can still bring a case for unfair dismissal if they have sufficient service. If probation is to be useful, it must bring with it a reasonable level of appraisal, support and training. The manager should have regular supervision with the new employee but should also pay more attention within it to raising any concerns and offering training and familiarisation for the work roles. Mentoring or 'buddying' with another member of staff may be helpful for the new worker. It is preferable that the same discipline, performance and notice procedures should apply to workers on probation – even within the period, it is only fair that they should have a right to put their views on what is said to be going wrong.

Supervision, appraisal and workforce development

Discipline is a negative way of managing people. Encouraging good work, developing skills, allowing people to learn from their mistakes and helping staff with their fears and blockages are all much more productive. These mechanisms are usually summed up in staff development, appraisal and training policies. The manager needs to take a positive view of staff development; it complements good supervision and appraisal. It is not just a nuisance because staff may be away on training or taking time to learn new ways of doing things.

Supervision of staff is one of the most important roles of the manager. In a factory, you might be able to manage by simply issuing instructions on tasks, work rotas or other practicalities. In a people-centred operation such as youth work, workers will need regular face-to-face discussion with their line manager about the progress of their work, priorities and actual or potential problems. Team meetings and informal discussions are not an adequate substitute. Supervision should normally be one to one. In a very few situations, pairs or very small groups may be appropriate where people do the same job but the manager should ensure that at some point staff have the opportunity for a supervision where they can raise individual concerns.

The manager needs to receive information about how the work is progressing, and any emerging issues such as stress or workload or particular young people that are causing concern. The manager will be monitoring the work, whether it is being completed and whether standards are satisfactory, but more importantly is responsible for helping to identify solutions to problems and creating a practical climate for change where improvement is necessary.

Dedicated time, preferably in a quiet and private situation, should be given to supervision and it should not be sacrificed to the pressures of other work. Both parties should prepare for the session by thinking about what has been achieved, what matters have arisen since the previous session and their objectives for dealing with problem areas. They should keep records of supervision, ideally as shared notes or forms with actions they agreed that each of them should take before the next session. If the manager does undertake to do something as a result of supervision, it is essential to follow that through. Supervision should be supportive, maybe developmental, and will generally be confidential apart from when others need to have information to deal with a particular issue. Supervision that reveals poor work practice may lead to disciplinary steps but it should never be confused with the disciplinary procedure itself. The manager needs to signal a clear transfer into a separate and formal procedure and should never start giving informal warnings.

There may be resistance to supervision in some situations where staff feel they have been doing the job a long time without interference or where there has been no tradition of individual supervision meetings. It is worth working at your own skills in supervision to be sure that you do offer something useful – the effort will be well repaid. You may wish to follow up some of the material on the skills involved (e.g., Hawkins and Shohet, 2007; Christian and Kitto, 1987; Adirondack, 2006, pp102–9).

Appraisal is a different activity. It is an occasional step back to look at such issues as how the job is going, whether the job description accurately describes the current role, learning needs, achievements, skills, how the worker can contribute to the agency priorities and how they see their own career progression. Most organisations use some form of appraisal and will issue their own guidance, which will tell you when appraisal meetings should take place, the sorts of questions that should be discussed and who should be informed of the outcomes. If you do not have such a set procedure, you should find time as a line manager to discuss their work as a whole with each worker you manage, in a way that goes beyond regular supervision. The manager needs to ensure that the system, 'the deal' for the member of staff, is absolutely transparent so that it can operate in a climate of reasonable trust. Appraisal is usually held annually but should be undertaken more often for new members of staff. Like supervision, it should result in concrete, agreed and recorded actions to be taken, including identification of training that is necessary or desirable.

Handy points out that at its best appraisal identifies skills and potential that can contribute to agency objectives, offers feedback on performance and helps to plan for the achievement of individual and collective targets. In some cases appraisal is used to determine pay rewards, though thankfully this is not common in the people-centred professions. Handy argues that these purposes can be contradictory. Members of staff will rarely openly admit to inadequate performance or skills when they think it will influence the work they are given or will have consequences for their progression. Most people will tailor their self-assessment to admit minor problems within an acceptable band of performance. Criticism only improves performance where it relates to particular issues or incidents *and* there is a genuine liking for the other person within a climate of trust – setting agreed achievable targets or positive feedback and praise for specific achievements are much more likely to help the employee to raise their game (Handy, 1999, pp225–8).

Your agency will probably have a staff or workforce development policy, which will set out arrangements for supervision and appraisal, access to training and development, and entitlements for both paid staff and volunteers to practical support such as time for training or travel expenses. If not, one should be produced. The training budget should relate to the system of identifying learning needs at appraisal and elsewhere and you will need to take into account essential training for particular staff such as first aid, child protection or database skills. It is important to remember that formal training is not the only route through which staff can develop their own competence. Other staff development opportunities may include shadowing, coaching, mentoring, learning groups, secondments or placements (Adirondack, 2006, pp118–23). It is good practice to encourage members of staff to have an agreed written development plan, which will include the identified learning needs, the activities by which they will be met, the learning objectives to be achieved, together with timescales and required resources.

The issue of support

Almost everybody needs to feel supported in their work. Support is different from supervision, although it should be an element of the supervisor's approach. Support can be provided by many different people inside and outside an organisation. It is not the sole province of the manager and it should be noted that managers themselves need support too. It is, however, the role of the manager to be sure that staff are finding the support they need to do the job effectively.

We would argue that there are two main dimensions to what is usually meant by support in this context. There is support in the sense of being understood and valued in your work, with the hopes, fears, achievements and disappointments that entails and there is also support in a crisis situation. We have already noted that a good manager will listen well, show that they notice extra effort or effective practice and give specific positive encouragement. Even a handwritten sticky note to thank a worker for a good piece of work will do wonders for morale. It is also important that staff can sound off or discuss personal issues in confidence. A box of tissues is essential management equipment! Crises can include the effects of stress; personal or family issues such as debt, divorce or bereavement; ill health or accidents. It may be appropriate to signpost the worker to specialist help or advice or to offer measures such as a temporarily reduced workload, increased flexibility of hours, compassionate leave or a phased return to work.

Managers in youth work, including the most senior service leads, also have a crucial role to play in the general support for the work. Youth work is very often misunderstood. The public, other professionals and sometimes politicians can be quick to criticise young people and those who work closely with them, if issues are not sorted out. Good managers will have a genuine feel of the process of youth work; they will understand that youth work is not about 'hit and run' methods of dealing with antisocial behaviour, crime or lack of achievement. They know it is about 'out-of-hours' work and a patient process of making contact, building relationships, creating boundaries and using that foundation for deliberately and sensitively offering opportunities for learning and personal development. Many other professional colleagues around us are also in for the long haul with young people but youth work precipitates misunderstanding with particular ease. The manager needs to communicate well to those outside the profession, advocate for both workers and young people and convey an understanding of their role to the paid staff and volunteers (discussed further in Chapter 2). Sometimes, the manager will need to provide the permission to take a measure of risk to reach young people in most need. An analogy may be helpful: the manager can act as an 'umbrella' to protect staff from the rain of outside criticism or misinterpretation. It also needs to be made clear to staff that the quid pro quo for that protection is that they keep the manager properly informed about their work and any potential problems.

Performance and discipline

Nobody wants to think about having to take disciplinary action against a member of staff. With good staff and appropriate supervision and support systems, you may be sufficiently fortunate to avoid it. Sometimes, however, things do go wrong and some action must be taken. There is one thing worse than a member of the team being well out of order and that is when nothing is done about it – the consequences affect everybody including our users.

The first thing to ask yourself on these occasions is whether you are looking at a disciplinary issue or a performance or capability matter. Disciplinary issues occur when the employee is deliberately and knowingly doing things that are wrong in the sense that they harm the organisation or other people or, in a youth work context, hurt young people in some way. There is often a list of behaviour typically regarded as deserving discipline in the organisation's disciplinary procedure. What is included will depend on the agency context. It will include such obvious issues as stealing or hitting someone (usually these are classed as gross misconduct) but it can also cover bad working practices such as poor timekeeping, failing to follow required procedures or undermining the organisation. The response to the poor behaviour of the worker will depend on its severity and most disciplinary procedures will have an escalating system of formal warnings and sanctions that can culminate in dismissal.

Performance matters, on the other hand, occur when the member of staff wants to do the job well but lacks the necessary knowledge, skills or competence to perform it well. Capacity issues arise when the member of staff cannot perform their job for other reasons such as prolonged absence from ill health.

The detailed route through the procedures usually diverges somewhat at this point but certain general principles apply. First, you need to be clear who is directly accountable to you in the management structure and therefore where you are responsible for taking action when things are going badly and where you need to alert somebody else. Second, act as early as possible – don't let it build up. If workers can claim they have been behaving this way for a very long time and nobody has said anything, it makes the case for acting much more difficult and the solutions harder to find. Third, make careful records of what went wrong and everything you do from the beginning (including dates); you will need these records for any formal hearing or appeal. And finally, take advice; the law is complex and action to deal with problems frequently fails because the manager did not take advice from human resources or a legal adviser before plunging ahead.

CASE STUDY

Care and attention: resolving personnel problems
Janet was a caretaker at a large youth centre. Her duties included moving tables and chairs and some large items such as the mats for the martial arts class. Unfortunately she had hurt her back quite badly and had now been absent with back pain for over nine months. Lifting was a particular problem. The youth worker at the centre was very concerned because he could not return his staffing to full complement or replace her while she was off sick but there was no apparent prospect of her returning in the foreseeable future.

The senior manager arranged a meeting with Janet under the local authority's sickness absence procedures and medical reports were requested from her GP. The manager explained to Janet that if her doctor thought the back problems would be continuing, there was a problem over her capacity to do her job. In the course of the interview, he discovered that Janet was desperately hanging on to her job despite having no real hope of a change in her fitness solely because she felt that she did not have enough pension accumulated to be able to afford to take ill-health retirement.

The manager explained to Janet that the job still needed to be done and that they needed to review all the possible options together including redeployment into another post. Janet felt she had no other skills and was very worried about her future as a result. Careful exploration, however, revealed that Janet had worked on the checkout at a major supermarket many years before and that she had good numeracy skills and some keyboard skills.

The care in investigating the problem and the attention to Janet's perceptions paid off. Agreement was reached that Janet should retrain taking a typing course. She is now working happily at a community centre in the same authority as an administrative assistant and is responsible amongst other things for data input on the records of classes and attendances.

ACTIVITY **4.2**

Sandra has been in post for just over a month working as receptionist and administrator. She is responsible to the manager of a large youth project. Her duties include answering the phone, maintaining mailing lists, filing and typing letters or reports. Sandra seems eager to help but two people have mentioned that she is a bit 'offhand' with callers on the phone. Also her typing is inaccurate and her manager has been forced to send nearly every task back for substantial correction.

If you were Sandra's manager would you:

- *initiate discipline;*

- *start a performance procedure;*

- *talk to her about her manner and mistakes;*

- *wait until nearer the end of her probationary period, when you know she can still be dismissed without appeal?*

Whether you embark on a performance or a disciplinary procedure, both are discipline processes in legal terms and may lead eventually to dismissal. Such processes have to be fair to the employee and are often described as subject to 'natural justice', which basically means that someone has a right to know what they are alleged to have done wrong, have access to the information being used against them and have an opportunity to answer the allegations. The law has now enshrined such principles in codes for employers to follow.

The complex Statutory Dismissal and Disciplinary Procedure (DDP) that came into force in 2004 has recently been replaced by a new ACAS Code of Practice. Failure to follow the code will not make a dismissal automatically unfair but a tribunal will be able to increase or decrease awards by up to 25 per cent if they feel either the employer or the employee has been unreasonable in failing to follow the recommended procedure (Rees, 2008).

The new ACAS Code of Practice on Disciplinary Procedures suggests that the following main principles should be followed in discipline or grievance cases (ACAS, 2009). They embody the principles of fairness to the employee.

- Issues should be dealt with promptly.

- Employers should act consistently, treating similar cases in the same way.

- Appropriate investigations should always be made to get the facts of the situation.

- Wherever possible, discipline or grievance processes should not be conducted by the manager who is immediately involved in the dispute.

- Where it is a matter of performance, however, the immediate manager should be involved.

- The employee should know the basis of the case against them and should always have the opportunity to put their side before any decision is taken.

- Employees have a right in law to be accompanied (by a friend, colleague or Trade Union representative) to formal discipline or grievance meetings.

- There should always be a right of appeal against the decision.

Suspension is also a disciplinary sanction and is normally adopted for suspected gross misconduct where continuing at work is a risk either to other people or financially. As a manager, you need to be familiar with the procedures and know what decisions you are able to take yourself and where you must involve other people.

Situations do occasionally occur where the conduct of a member of staff is dangerous or out of control. For example, you might be on a residential and find a worker has started a fight and injured one of the young people. If you can do so, ask for advice from a senior manager. If you are unable to speak to someone more senior or the risk must be more urgently contained, you should suspend the member of staff immediately and send them home. This gives time for the proper procedure and investigation. Do not be tempted to tell them that they are dismissed.

Leadership

You do not have to be a manager to be a leader (as you will probably have seen in many situations). A 'jobsworth' manager is undoubtedly not a leader but the two roles are inextricably linked and the effective manager will show leadership qualities. It is your task as a manager both to lead and to create a functioning team. Mullins argues that leadership is essentially 'a relationship through which one person influences the behaviour or actions of other people' (Mullins, 2007, p363). Adair suggests that the leader works to reconcile the need to get the task done, the team maintenance needs and the needs of the individual in order to produce effective action (Adair, 1979). The leader is inextricably related to the team and the individuals within it.

Leadership styles vary and many volumes have been filled on theoretical models to determine which style works best in particular work situations. Undoubtedly this matters; we all know that if the fire alarm goes off, it is not a good idea to have a meeting to consult about the best exit route. On the other hand, it is also inadvisable to try to switch your own natural style of leadership completely to suit different scenarios. Most workers get unsettled and start questioning the honesty of the presentation (see Chapter 2) if their manager's style keeps changing. An awareness of the strengths and weaknesses of your own approach and a willingness to make less radical adaptations is probably the best way forward. If you want to read more about how leadership styles impact on the effectiveness of the manager, there are good summaries of the theories of leadership in the texts by Mullins (2007) and Handy (1999).

ACTIVITY 4.3

Think about the individuals working at your placement situation or your workplace.

- *What do you think motivates each person?*

- *What do they need from their job?*

- *What do they get out of coming to work?*

- *How could a manager harness those needs and motivations to make the youth work more effective?*

In considering leadership style, there are some points that relate particularly to youth and community work that are worth remembering. We believe in empowering and involving young people. The manager needs to model that approach and therefore it is unlikely that an undiluted authoritarian approach will work with staff. Youth workers themselves are often slightly unorthodox or anti-authority and that is one reason why they relate well to young people. They will work best if they are consulted and empowered themselves. They need to understand what is going on – communication is key.

You need to be clear, however, on the limits to consultation. Decisions need to be made and your room for flexibility may be constrained. The manager also needs to make crystal clear what is an absolute requirement: what 'just has to be done' and is not the subject for debate. This might, for instance, apply to health and safety law or monitoring requirements for Comprehensive Area Assessment or for funding bodies. Follow through your instruction and make sure there is action if it is not completed – there is little point in instructions that everybody knows people do not follow.

Many youth workers would be described as charismatic leaders. Their power and influence resides in their personality and who they are. They are colourful, imaginative, fun to be with, they have tales to tell. Young people are attracted to them. Such workers may struggle with a management role. Charisma can put others in the shade rather than developing them; it tends to attract followers not people who can think for themselves. It is useful for conveying a vision but unless there is the competence and persistence to implement the ideas, the vision just evaporates.

It may also be a surprise to you to discover how much effect on people a leader (or manager) can have. Authority, power and status go with the role (often but not always progressively greater with progress up the hierarchy). The new manager suddenly picks up those attributes. Remember you will no longer be just one of the team – there will now be a distance between you and other workers (see Chapter 1). Small actions can have considerable impact; even such minute detail as not saying 'good morning' to people. Think about how much it is appreciated when the youth officer bothers to come to the end of project show or your director turns up to hand out certificates. Consider the negative effect when a manager often comes in late and models a lack of commitment. Your planning and choice of style needs to take account of this move into the leadership position.

ACTIVITY 4.4

Tannenbaum and Schmidt offer a classic continuum of leadership styles.

- *Some managers* tell *people to implement the decisions they have made.*

- *Others make their decisions,* sell *them to others and seek to persuade them to accept it.*

- *Some* consult *the group, presenting the problem and only deciding what to do after hearing views and potential solutions.*

- *Some managers* join *the group. They spot the problem, explain the constraints to the group and then join the group as a member in making the decision (Tannenbaum and Schmidt, 1973; Mullins, 2007, pp372–4).*

Reflect on your own natural leadership style. How would you describe it?

Can you think of a situation where you might need to adapt it to get things done?

Teamwork

Youth work managers will relate to several teams. Their own staff team is the most obvious but they are also likely to be part of a corporate or senior management team in their own organisation and committees and partnership groups elsewhere. They have primary responsibility for leading their own staff to ensure appropriate delivery to young people.

All teams are groups and many volumes have been written on group functioning and group work theory, much of which you will have considered in your own group work training. This can easily be over-simplified as if the models apply in all groups but youth work managers can draw on this skill set in establishing a working team (see the summary on the workings of groups in Handy, 1999, pp150–79; Mullins, 2007, pp330–57). Effective teams are, however, more than just groups – they will show characteristics of working well together such as having clear and shared objectives, understanding each other's roles, supporting others, communicating well, using people's skills well and resolving differences constructively.

- Teams need people to take different roles. Where people are too alike, the team is not generally effective – so differences are no bad thing. Belbin's work outlines typical roles, subsequently adapted by many others, such as the 'Innovator' who produces ideas and imaginative proposals, the 'Fixer' who has useful contacts and is good at getting resources or the 'Finisher' who is task centred and makes sure the deadlines are met and the job is done (Belbin, 1981; and see www.businessballs.com). The manager needs to value these different contributions but ensure that individuals do not get boxed into a role they do not want.

- The manager needs to balance task and maintenance functions. Workers do need to be clear about overall objectives, essential procedures and what their exact role is in the sessions with young people. The manager needs to distribute tasks to ensure an overall result and work with the team to solve the problems that arise. At the same time feelings need to be acknowledged, disillusion and anger need to be aired, people need encouragement, conflicts may need to be resolved. A handy rule of thumb is to let people 'whinge' but not for more than ten minutes and then make sure the team moves on to what can be done about it and the tasks ahead.

- The manager will need to ensure that some maintenance activities take place. A meal out or the leaving party for a colleague are good opportunities to thank people and build a sense of belonging. Team-building exercises may be worthwhile. Teams need a certain level of cohesiveness to function effectively but not to the extent that harmony, 'groupthink' or even friendships are allowed to overtake rationality – beware of developing cohesion into an unprofessional clique.

- Teams establish norms amongst themselves (see Chapter 3 on culture). The manager needs to set high standards of professional behaviour. The team leader, for instance, who is always late for the meeting, is never prepared and not infrequently turns up with a hangover is not a good model for the group.

- Support for each other in youth work teams is critical. Situations with young people can be annoying, testing or even dangerous. It is crucial that youth work teams should thrash out expectations of each other and of the young people. Young people should preferably be part of the decisions about boundaries. It is then imperative that staff should back each other up on issues of boundaries and behaviour.

- Give other people credit for what they achieve and do well. This is a cardinal rule of good teamwork and applies to external partnerships as well as to in-house teams. The manager who takes credit without acknowledging the contribution of colleagues or other organisations does real damage to the willingness to work together.

Dealing with conflict

You may well have disagreements with individuals on your team; you may feel angry about poor performance or some particular incident. Other people at the workplace may be at loggerheads for similar reasons. If these conflicts are sufficiently severe to disrupt the work, make people unhappy, or block team functioning, they need to be dealt with. It is best to avoid terms such as 'personality clash' – they just cover up whatever is at issue. Focus on the behaviour that is causing the problem or what actually happened in the incident. Do not opt out – try to work through the problem assertively, without manipulating the other person into agreement or withdrawal. This will mean acknowledging your own needs and feelings, being accurate and specific with the other person, explaining the effect of their behaviour, being specific and reasonable about what you want to change, taking on board the other person's viewpoint and reasoning (Dainow and Bailey, 1988). Use any points on which you can agree; if things are stuck, recap; keep working for agreement on the problem, causes, solutions, and actions to be taken. The same principles of being specific about the behaviour, acknowledging its effect, identifying options and searching for the points of agreement will apply if you are helping other people or even groups to resolve conflicts.

The manager needs to own their personal feelings but this does not necessarily mean showing them on all occasions. We have already observed that the leadership position gives added force to what you communicate to others. You may feel angry but you do not need to show anger. You may feel disappointed but you do not have to sulk. Your feelings are a signal for your own information but you should be in control of what is spewed out on others. If you find you cannot keep this control, you may sometimes need to find support to talk through these emotions outside the workplace. Promotion to a management role does not mean that you cease to need support yourself.

C H A P T E R   R E V I E W

This chapter underlines the following issues.

- People management is complex. Take advice and take procedures seriously – they are not there just for show.

- Meticulous attention to good recruitment and induction processes pays dividends down the line.

- Part-time and casual staff should be properly valued. It is not just a matter of sticking to legal requirements but of recognising and developing quality practice amongst workers who are often the backbone of youth work provision.

- If equality of opportunity for staff is truly embedded in the workplace, the quality and inclusiveness of the youth work practice will be enhanced in parallel.

- Supervision of staff is one of your key roles. It needs to be regular and systematic and given adequate time.

- Positive, constructive feedback and encouragement are nearly always a more effective route to improving staff performance than discipline.

- If things have gone badly wrong and discipline is necessary, act sooner rather than later – take advice on the correct procedure, and always keep a detailed record of the steps you took.

- Leadership is about influencing the behaviour of your team. You need to consider your own leadership style and how best to use it to get the job done and meet the needs of your staff at the same time.

- The manager cannot just be 'one of the team'. With promotion to the role, you will have gained in authority, power and status to some degree. Be aware of that in how you treat your staff.

- Cultivate your team. The support and back up you all give each other is a critical factor in surviving the pressures of youth work.

Adirondack, S (2006) *Just about managing? Effective management for voluntary organisations and community groups.* London: London Voluntary Service Council.

Doherty, T and Horne, T (2002) *Managing public services.* London: Routledge.

Handy, C (1999) *Understanding organisations.* London: Penguin Books; particulary pages 96–122 about how leadership styles impact on the effectiveness of the manager.

Mullins, L (2007) *Management and organisational behaviour,* 8th edition. Harlow: Financial Times/ Prentice Hall; particularly pages 362–403 on leadership styles.

Hawkins, P and Shohet, R (2007) *Supervision in the helping professions,* 3rd edition. Maidenhead: Open University Press.

www.acas.org.uk

www.equalityhumanrights.com

www.volunteering.org.uk

ACAS (2005) *Getting it right – recruitment and section* (leaflet). London: ACAS Publications. Online: www.acas.org.uk/CHttpHandler.ashx?id=283&p=0

ACAS (2007) *Tackling discrimination and promoting equality.* London: ACAS Publications. Online: www.acas.org.uk

ACAS (2009) *Discipline and grievances at work* (leaflet). London: ACAS Publications. Online: www.acas.org.uk/CHttpHandler.ashx?id=1043

ACAS (2009) *Code of practice on grievance and discipline.* London: ACAS Publications. Online: http://www.acas.org.uk/CHttpHandler.ashx?id=1047&p=0

Adair, J (1979) *Action-centred leadership.* Aldershot: Gower.

Adirondack, S (2006) *Just about managing? Effective management for voluntary organisations and community groups.* London: London Voluntary Service Council.

Argyris, C (1960) *Understanding organizational behaviour.* Chicago: Dorsey Press.

Belbin, R (1981) *Management teams.* London: Heinemann.

Business Link. (2007) *Prevent discrimination and value diversity.* Online: www.businesslink.gov.uk

Christian, C and Kitto, J (1987) *The theory and practice of supervision*, London: YMCA George Williams College.

Dainow, S and Bailey, C (1988) *Developing skills with people: training for person to person client contact.* Chichester: John Wiley.

Hawkins, P and Shohet, R (2007) *Supervision in the helping professions*, 3rd edition. Maidenhead: Open University Press.

Handy, C (1999) *Understanding organisations.* London: Penguin Books.

Hoggarth, L and Smith, D (2004) *Understanding the impact of Connexions on young people at risk.* Nottingham: DfES Publications.

IDS: Incomes Data Services Ltd (2001) *Continuity of employment: employment law handbook.* London: IDS.

Merton, B et al. (2004) *An evaluation of the impact of youth work in England.* Nottingham: DfES Publications.

Mullins, L (2007) *Management and organisational behaviour,* 8th edition. Harlow: Financial Times/ Prentice Hall.

Rees, L (2008) 'Legal Q & A, Employment Bill 2007', *Personnel Today*, January. Online: **www.personneltoday.com/articles/2008/01/14/4367/legal-q.html**

Tannenbaum, R and Schmidt, W (1973) 'How to choose a leadership pattern', *Harvard Business Review*, May–June: 162–75, 178–80.

Volunteering England *Should we have a volunteering agreement?* Question sheet 41. Online: **www.volunteering.org.uk/Resources/information**

Chapter 5
Managing resources

Liz Hoggarth

Achieving your Youth and Community Work degree

This chapter is about the essential skills of managing finance and other resources in order to achieve high-quality youth work. It will help you to meet the following National Occupational Standards (February 2008).

- *1.2.2 Work with young people to manage resources for youth work activities*

- *2.4.1 Fulfil the legal, regulatory and ethical requirements relevant to youth work*

- *2.4.2 Ensure that youth work activities comply with legal, regulatory and ethical requirements*

- *5.4.1 Make sure your own actions reduce risks to health and safety*

- *5.4.2 Ensure health and safety requirements are met in your area of responsibility*

Introduction

Many youth workers do not enjoy the aspects of the job that concern managing finance, buildings and equipment; they prefer the direct work with young people. Yet without such resources the face-to-face youth work cannot take place. If this part of management is approached positively, it can make a huge difference to the amount of provision available to young people and to the quality of their experience. This chapter covers basic guidance on the meaning of accountability and delegation, setting a budget and monitoring spend. It also looks at the management of buildings to maximise their use and accessibility and continues with an examination of the health and safety duties of the youth work manager and the tasks of managing other resources such as equipment or vehicles.

Managing money

The manager's role in financial management

Depending on your work situation, your financial management responsibilities may be for as little as claiming your own expenses and ordering stationery when you need it or as much as several hundred thousand pounds for a project with a team of full-time staff or even several million as an area manager in a big authority. The principles are exactly the same – as the manager you need to be able to account for the money you use, know what your powers are to spend money, how much money is available, how much has been used and is likely to be used, and be certain that spend is legal and honest.

Accountability

In the youth work field, you will almost always be handling public money, that is, money from other people's taxes or donations. You may work in a business or social enterprise organisation but it will generally be 'not for profit', that is, one that is not making money for individuals. The funds may come to you as grants from a charity or trust or government body or as a service level agreement or contract from a local authority or another public service provider. They are not yours to spend as you wish; you need to be able to show that they were spent wisely for the purpose for which they were given and to have records of how they were spent. Financial responsibility and accountability mean knowing what your organisation wants to achieve, how much it will cost and where that money is coming from. You will probably need to bring in some income, and your agency should not be taking on commitments that it cannot meet. Your organisation needs to be sure it can pay invoices and they should be paid on time. You will need records and reports to show that there is a planned budget and that expenditure is in line with that or corrective action is being taken. Charities will need accounts that are independently examined or audited (see Adirondack, 2006, pp207–20 for an outline of financial requirements in voluntary organisations). In public organisations there are usually internal auditors who may call in accounts or particular spending commitments for examination at any time.

Delegation and financial authority

As a manager coming into post, you will want to be clear about what level of financial authority you hold (normally spelled out in the financial regulations) – otherwise you could soon find yourself in hot water. You may be responsible for planning particular budgets or for contributing your views to the planning cycle or you may simply be told what your budget is.

In most organisations there will also be limits on what spend you can authorise or sign for without the agreement of somebody higher up in the hierarchy. In a local authority, the scheme of who is responsible for each level of finance is often called the 'delegations'. A senior worker at a youth project, for instance, might be able to order equipment up to the value of £5000 without further permission and a service director may be authorised to sign off contracts worth millions. In most voluntary organisations, the treasurer will have a role in authorising major expenditure. It is necessary to be clear – partly to protect your own reputation for efficiency and partly because you need to understand how to get spending decisions authorised.

There will also be limits on your ability to spend certain designated sums for other purposes. The main division in most budgets is between 'capital' and 'revenue'. Capital is money for one-off, usually major, commitments such as new buildings, vehicles or large equipment purchases. Revenue means everyday expenditure on running costs and service delivery such as staff salaries, rent, heat and light, insurance or activity costs. The general rule with a very few technical exceptions is that you cannot use capital for revenue purposes and vice versa; this implies that great care is needed to ensure, for example, that capital grants are only used for capital items.

Some monies, especially in a voluntary organisation, may be earmarked for particular purposes. 'Reserves' are savings kept to tide the organisation over in a time of crisis or a gap in funding or sometimes to pay redundancy if the project has to close. From time to time, the Charity Commission recommends keeping certain levels of reserves and the youth work manager will not be able to use these funds for ongoing work. Other funds may be termed 'restricted' funds, with their special purpose spelled out such as extending the building or replacing the minibuses and again these are not available for general use.

Most grants and commissions now come with set objectives, often with specific outcomes to be achieved. Some are very narrow in their purpose. The manager needs to have a system for accounting separately for each grant and must make sure it is spent in line with its objectives. Your bookkeeper or accountant can advise on how each grant should be 'coded' to keep the relevant orders and invoices separate. Never 'borrow' from one grant to fill a gap in another – that will almost certainly result in financial meltdown and if the confusion is picked up, grants may be withdrawn. It is also unacceptable to 'double count'. That means claiming money twice for the same expenditure on a piece of work.

In an ordinary revenue budget, you may have some freedom to 'vire' money from one heading to another. For instance, you may have too much money for printing and stationery and want to spend it on craft materials or casual staffing. The rules for 'virement', how you may or may not move money between the headings of the budget, will be available in your organisation and if not, your board needs to decide what is allowable.

Finally, you may not be allowed to carry money that has not been used in one year into the next financial year. This is very often the case and local authority rules have become stricter in recent years. You may be able to use 'liabilities', which are usually taken to mean goods ordered in one financial year and received early in the next before close down of accounts. In other cases, the funding body may be prepared to agree to carry over. Watch for spending that is getting behind the project timetable as 'slippage' will almost inevitably mean that young people lose out on resources that could be available to them.

Setting a budget

The budget for a unit as a whole or for a special project within it is simply a device for summing up where the money comes from (income) and what it is spent on (expenditure). Annual accounts are a constitutional or legal requirement for voluntary organisations and public bodies. Members of the public are entitled to see them. They do not, however, provide the current picture.

In most projects, the management budget will deal with what is available for the financial year but will also divide that up on a monthly or quarterly basis so that you can track the financial situation. The budget will have headings for different types of outlay such as building maintenance, equipment or staffing so that where spending is going can be analysed. In many organisations, these headings will be set for you but you still need to understand what they cover and be sure that you know that the things you need for the work with young people can be coded to one or other of these analysis headings. Typically project budgets do not include all the items you need. You may need to earmark budgets for particular needs such as the building and its regular maintenance, activities with the young people, health and safety requirements such as electrical testing, staff development and training, or insurance. You should make sure sufficient insurance is in place; some categories of insurance are essential, namely Employer's Liability, Public Liability, building and contents insurance.

Budgets may include 'in kind' contributions such as volunteer time or administrative support. These will be balanced off against an equal part of the budgeted spend. You do, however, need to be sure that you can justify and account for these items and show evidence that the contribution did take place (for example, in volunteer hours committed at the estimated equivalent for paid staff).

ACTIVITY 5.1

You want to start a youth project to reach disaffected young people in your ward and introduce them to recreational activities and accredited training. Your manager and the treasurer prepared an outline budget some time ago, as set out below. Try not to glaze over. Before the grant applications are submitted, you want to check that they have allowed for everything needed.

Make a list of the sorts of things you will need to spend money on and check it against the provisional budget.

- *Do the headings cover what you might need to work with the young people or do you need others?*
- *Are they all necessary?*
- *Are any essentials missing?*
- *Do the figures and the proportions between different items reflect what you would want to see on such a project?*
- *Can any of the items be the subject of an application for one-off capital grants?*

Youth Outreach Project Budget Full Year 09/10

Income		
Grants (Source 1)	136000	
Grants (Source 2)	60000	
In Kind	3000	
Miscellaneous	200	
Total income		199200
Expenditure		
Staff costs		
Gross salaries (FT and PT)	86000	
NI & pension (@20%)	17200	

Training	2200	
Recruitment	1000	
Subsistence	600	
Staff Travel	2000	
Total staff costs		109000
Premises, office and equipment		
Rent and rates	3500	
Furniture	1000	
Repairs and maintenance	800	
Cleaning	1500	
Utilities (heat and light)	800	
Telephone and mobile phones	3000	
Stationery	400	
Computers, internet and software	1800	
IT support	500	
Photocopying/printing	5000	
Postage	500	
Office sundries and miscellaneous	600	
Health and safety	600	
Total premises and equipment		20000
Insurances		
Employer's liability	1400	
Public liability	1400	
Additional life insurance	400	
Total insurances		3200
Activity costs (casual staff, volunteer costs, young people's travel, activities/residentials, minor equipment)		
Activity expenditure	30000	
In kind contributions	3000	
Total activity costs		33000
Management charges		
Management charges (at 10% approx.)	19000	
Total management/support charges		19000
Evaluation		
External evaluation	10000	
Technical support	5000	
Total evaluation & support costs		15000
Total Expenditure		199200
Net Surplus/Deficit		0

Your budget may need to be 'profiled'. This means anticipating the ups and downs likely in each month of the financial year and gearing the specific monthly budget to that profile rather than dividing equally by 12. For example, you may be running holiday schemes in the summer and will have more expenditure during those months and use most of the grants gained for that purpose. In this case, it is pointless worrying that previously the heading is underspent or that in the summer months it is more than expected for the average monthly period. If your budget is not designed in this way, you still need to bear in mind the expected variations over the year when you monitor and assess spend. Linked to this profiling is the importance of having a cash flow budget that anticipates both the expenditure and the income so you can ensure that there is enough money available to pay for your commitments in any particular month. For some organisations that could mean negotiating a loan until the next payment from the funders is due to arrive if there is going to be a particularly expensive period. Do not forget to allow for the cost of that loan.

Ideally the budget should be planned after a review of the work and a good look at future needs. There are numerous management devices for reviewing future strategy and the operating context of the organisation and relating that to financial requirements such as using a SWOT (Strengths, Weaknesses, Opportunities and Threats) or SPELT analysis (Social, Political, Economic, Legal and Technical) or 'zero-based' budgeting. Field argues that while organisational objective setting, service delivery planning and budget planning are often divorced from each other, those processes ought to be firmly linked. He also suggests that it is important to be clear that budget reductions cannot normally be achieved year on year without reductions in quality or quantity of service and that managers should be prepared to spell out those consequences (Field, 2007, pp56–70).

In most organisations, however, the budget headings stay the same and the budget is expected to be similar, with the addition of inflation and any new grants and the subtraction of any budget cuts required. Even if budgeting is done in this way in your agency, it is good practice for you as a youth work manager to think through the current needs and the whole organisation ought to take time to review periodically. Finance should be pro-actively related to the planning of the programme. You may, for instance, have an influx of Somali families in your neighbourhood and need to ask what youth work provision and outreach their young people are likely to need. If you are serious about including them in provision, then your budget will need to reflect the answer. You may know that your youth group could get much more out of producing their newsletter with some new but costly computer software and that they really ought to be offered accreditation for their learning from the activity. That will require new fundraising or accommodation in your existing budget. If some of the young people need anger management sessions, do you have the skills in house or will you need to bring in a facilitator? What will that cost? Who will cover other sessions if you use an existing member of staff? What about rooms, travel costs for the young people, worksheets or video equipment? Such factors have budget implications – you may be able to apply for new grants or budget to spend less on a part of the provision that is not currently well used. Being realistic is obviously an important part of helping young people learn to make decisions but programming should drive the use of the budget and not vice versa. If your budget is always viewed as a reason why things cannot be done, you are not managing it effectively.

Many managers make a mystery out of the budget either to bolster their own importance and power, as an excuse why things cannot be done, or to exclude staff from decision making. In the youth work context, this will ripple through to the way that young people are treated. There may be isolated reasons for discretion on financial matters but these rarely justify this approach. Your managers or board in a voluntary project need to be fully informed of any problems that emerge and staff need to have information about the finances. Staff who understand how the budget works, how and why they need to account for it, what the income targets are and why some resources are difficult to find will generally be more constructive and cooperative than those who are kept in the dark. They may well have good ideas on how to raise funds or make savings. They can be more realistic and can more easily help young people to learn responsibility for money. Senior managers of youth provision and targeted services for young people need to consult their staff. Even if they are not ultimately responsible for budget planning, they will have an awareness of where needs are emerging and local opportunities for funding and partnership work. Commitment will be increased and stress will be reduced.

Monitoring spending

Whatever the size of your budget, you need to know how much is being spent against it. You will also want to know how much has been spent under each heading so that overspend can be reined in before it is too late. This chapter does not set out to explain how to record income and expenditure, keep cash books, reconcile bank statements or set up petty cash systems. There are useful guides available on these topics (NCVO, 2007; Finance hub, 2008; the DCSF FMSiS (Financial Management Standard in Schools) site) and local authorities and voluntary organisations will usually offer their own guidance on systems. Appropriate software can also help you.

Make an ally of your finance officer or treasurer, show an intelligent interest in the accounts and discuss them frequently. Do not let a project administrator or bookkeeper take over so that you are not aware of what is happening financially – that is a recipe for trouble. If you find budget sheets bewildering, Field has helpful advice on how to understand what the information means (Field, 2007, pp78–81). There are some common sense measures you can take so that you know what is going on financially.

- Ensure that invoices, salary and expense claims are paid regularly and that items are entered up into the accounts system at least weekly and preferably daily.

- Examine the spend in detail every month. Large organisations will provide managers with statements or electronic access to accounts; effective voluntary organisations, however small, will examine monthly spend with members of their board. Some organisations will be using 'cost commitment' accounting systems and that means that you will also get a statement of what has been committed but not yet paid (such as new computers that are ordered but have not yet arrived and been paid for). In any case, you need to take account of any major commitments you have made if they do not yet show up in the accounts.

- Keep an eye on 'variance'. The term means the difference between the budgeted spend at this point in the year and the actual spend. For instance, sending out a new publicity leaflet to the whole mailing list may have seriously dented the stationery budget and variance will be showing up. You could adjust that later by economising on photocopying or reducing the number of leaflets in the year. You might have an underspend on staffing showing up because of vacancies and might be able to argue for using that for part-time staffing. It is good practice to adopt a rule of thumb that you will go into detail in order to find out exactly what is going on wherever variance is plus or minus more than a certain figure, say 5 or 10 per cent overspend or underspend against the expected spend at that point.

- Remember to look ahead. Will there be activity costs or bills in a future month for which you need to ensure that money is retained?

- Crucially, if you are out of your depth or in a muddle, ask for help sooner rather than later. Do not drift on hoping it will sort itself out in time.

Probity

As a manager, you need to make sure that money is spent honestly and on the things that are necessary to achieve the outcomes you want with young people. We can all point to instances of workers on expensive conferences that did not really provide information or skills needed for the job or crazy spending at the end of the financial year on equipment that no one really needs. Everybody involved in youth work, whatever their level, has a responsibility to make sure the money they spend is properly accounted for and contributes in some way to serving young people effectively.

'Probity' means uprightness, honesty and systems that are not easily corrupted or misused. It is often applied to the financial arrangements of organisations. There are several elements of practice usually applied to make systems less open to abuse. Most agencies will have a set of financial regulations which details these rules and levels of authority. The Charity Commission sets down financial standards for voluntary organisations with charitable status and in some cases agencies will also be companies limited by guarantee registered with Companies House. The annual accounts and records of directors that need to be returned are aimed at ensuring probity in charity and company operation.

In day-to-day practice, receipts should be supplied for what employees or volunteers spend and in most cases these should detail VAT paid. If you are claiming expenses or money for purchases, you need your own system for keeping and recording receipts. Your unit should normally have a petty cash system with known limits and receipts for expenditure and staff should never borrow from the float. Petty cash should be regularly accounted for and independently checked. Where young people or volunteers are paid very small amounts for expenses (bus fares, for example) an internal form that says what the claim was for and is dated and signed by the recipient is usually sufficient.

Nobody should have access to spending or claiming money without an independent check. Orders over a set level should normally be countersigned and two people should sign for 'goods received'; this should ensure that fraudulent or unnecessary orders for goods or services cannot be processed. Cheques should always be signed by at least two people or there may be a computer system that generates payments that will need a second authorisation. Computerised financial records should always be backed up. Bank accounts for clubs and projects should never be held in the name of an individual. The signatories (more than one signatory is good practice) should be agreed by the board or with the local authority, and the accounts of small units within a parent organisation, such as youth clubs operating one or two nights a week, should be periodically inspected.

Workers should also be prepared to account for their time, which is also an expensive resource. Youth work often operates at a distance from the management core and often in the evenings or weekends. It works on trust but some basic systems are necessary to ensure that the staff work the hours they are paid for and that basic ratios and safety requirements are covered. An appropriate time recording system that is not over complicated helps to defend the service against allegations that workers are not available when they should be or providing proper value for their salary costs.

Managing buildings

The building as a resource

Many 'people workers' dislike having responsibility for premises. Most of the people we want to reach will, however, end up needing a building at some point – to meet and talk, to do activities or to plan joint action. Buildings are a precious resource.

For this reason, buildings should be as open and accessible as possible and this may also provide a source of income. The youth work manager will be seeking to ensure that access without jeopardising the flexibility and tolerance that young people need. If buildings are shared, your job is one of negotiating agreements and boundaries. If you have building management in your direct responsibilities, you will need to ensure that the building is clean and safe and you may need caretaking to cater for a range of users. Opening hours, the booking system and telephone numbers should be clear, reliable and well advertised. You will need to work to make disability access a reality.

Ancillary staff such as cleaners or caretakers are an essential part of your team. They should be valued and acknowledged. If they are properly included in the 'mission' of the agency to serve young people and thanked for their contribution, they are much more likely to respond warmly to young people and carry out their role effectively. In one youth and community organisation, the maintenance team was included in the staff conferences and in target setting. They not only began to see their maintenance work as important to the feel and efficiency of the whole place but also started to take young people for training schemes in construction and maintenance.

Maintenance

If you are managing a building, try to think of it as an advertisement rather than a burden. Given the age and quality of some community buildings, this can be a real struggle but tolerating a dirty and unattractive building often starts a vicious circle of declining usage and failure to bring in new resources. The state of the lavatories is a very fair indicator of how well a building is managed!

The ideal is to have a budget for regular maintenance (such as painting the exterior or renewing window frames) as well as an allocation for emergency repairs. In a local authority, these funds may well be held centrally and a good relationship with technical services staff (or whatever the relevant department may be) is essential. In a voluntary organisation, such funds must be created and jealously guarded for their purpose.

There are steps you can take to augment resources for your building. Watch the running costs of the building – you may, for instance, be able to save by programming the heating better. Keep a weather eye on what is available in capital funding or regeneration schemes which might help. A new project, for instance, might apply not only for staffing but also for capital to refurbish a room or buy new equipment. Senior officers can support their staff by searching out such opportunities to create a steady drip feed of building renovation and improvements to disabled access.

Alternatively you may go for self-help in the form of volunteers, community service schemes or a joint project with the young people themselves. A new coat of paint, an eye-catching mural or maybe some new curtains can go a long way in making the place more welcoming. Make sure you have the necessary permissions for what you want to do and never attempt structural alterations yourself.

Managing health and safety

The youth worker has a critical role in managing health and safety. This affects every conceivable aspect of management – managing people, money, premises or equipment. Putting it negatively, if you let a member of staff get so pressured that it makes them ill, if you let young people travel in a badly maintained minibus, if you teach a dance routine without assessing the risks of injury, if someone trips on a loose carpet, then the question of liability arises. You may face reprimand, discipline or even (in mercifully rare circumstances) prosecution. Your organisation may have to pay compensation or fines, and in a few situations, where you knowingly failed to follow instructions or exercise good sense, you may be personally liable. A manager is responsible for assessing the risks and taking reasonable steps to reduce them.

Putting it positively, management of health and safety is part of creating the climate of trust – with young people, their parents, your staff and external bodies. Positive attitudes to health and safety can ensure that young people can experience challenge and some degree of risk, within a context of reasonable safety. You may well feel that health and safety requirements have gone over the top, that our society has become too 'risk averse' and too concerned about 'ambulance chasers'. There is an element of truth in this but nobody wants to return to the days when children suffered horrendous injuries working in factories, and closer to home, no one wants to see a young person badly injured in an accident at the youth club. It is a matter of taking a sensible practical approach. As the Chair of the Health and Safety Commission put it 'What I believe we as adults are charged with doing is helping children to understand that risks are there and how to deal with them NOT how to avoid them' (Judith Hackitt, October 2007).

Once again, plenty of training is available and there are helpful sources of guidance, most notably the excellent website of the Health and Safety Executive (HSE). The core of the Health and Safety at Work Act 1974 and subsequent legislation is that both the employer and the employees have a duty to prevent harm to those who work for them and those who use their services or visit the workplace. You must decide how health and safety issues will be managed – this is your 'health and safety policy'. Policies should be regularly reviewed and updated. You must then decide what could harm people, how serious the risk is and what steps you should take to prevent harm. That is 'risk assessment' and it applies to all aspects of the premises, all materials in use and every activity. Apply common sense: the law requires you to identify the hazards and do everything 'reasonably practical' to protect people, not to remove risk altogether. You must make sure the reasonable steps are implemented and that you keep records. If you have a sizeable number of people regularly working or meeting in a building, there should be alarm tests and fire practices and the dates should be recorded.

Youth work premises and projects should have an up-to-date file of risk assessments, any guidance on particular activities and their health and safety policy readily available. Local authorities will usually supply their projects with the relevant forms and policies; voluntary organisations can find templates on the HSE website.

There are a few further requirements under the law. You must display the health and safety law poster or give workers a leaflet. You must report certain categories of serious accidents. A new voluntary organisation that employs people will need to register either with the HSE or more usually the local authority. They must also take out Employer's Liability Compulsory Insurance (which covers claims from employees) and display the certificate (local authorities are exempt). It is advisable to inform your insurance company if you take students, volunteers, trainees or work experience placements. Staff should be provided with basic welfare facilities (such as washing and drinking water), free access to safety training, and a means of consultation on safety matters.

The law also requires a responsible person (usually the manager) to assess the needs for first aid. All workplaces require as a minimum an 'appointed person' who takes the role of looking after an injured employee, calling an ambulance and maintaining the first aid supplies. They will normally have completed an 'Emergency Aid in the Workplace' course. All youth work premises and minibuses should have a first aid kit. In the youth work situation you will also be responsible for young people and other users so 'first aiders' (who have completed an approved HSE course) may be necessary, especially if you have any high-risk activities.

Make health and safety a positive integral part of your planning, establish the procedures as routine, and it will become much easier. Accept that it is the manager's job to create the right climate of a sensible approach to risk and communicate that message to your staff.

Safeguarding

Apart from the physical risks to health and wellbeing, the manager is also responsible for ensuring that young people are safeguarded from adults who might wish to abuse them.

Your local authority is responsible overall for child protection and will offer guidance and training; voluntary organisations will have their own procedures which ensure communication to the right local authority officer where necessary (NCVYS, 2008).

Safeguarding has resource management dimensions. You will need a child protection procedure on file and available to staff. You may need to budget for Criminal Conviction Checks or staff training. You will need to think about the activities where it is necessary to have two members of staff or there are particular needs for male or female workers. Computers are a concern where either staff or young people have access. Appropriate rules for use should be in place and technical protection such as firewalls may be necessary. All filming and photographic displays carry risks; an innocent picture of a youth club performance might, for instance, give an abusive partner the clue they want about where to look for the child or young person. The permission of the individual or parents (for under-16s) should always be sought before any photographic material is used or filming is allowed at events.

Managing other resources

Youth work managers will be responsible for a range of other resources and they or their staff will need to identify and gather what is needed for projects and activities with the young people. This area can easily be neglected and can give rise to real and often unexpected problems. Some pointers are listed below.

- This is an opportunity to involve young people and help them learn responsibility and practical skills. Even for small-scale activities, they can be involved in drawing up a budget for a project or event (such as a dance showcase or creating their own allotment). They can identify and help source the equipment and materials needed. This can help them to make realistic judgements, manage money, stay within financial and legal limits, make a case to outsiders or look after equipment. Where appropriate these skills could be entered on records of learning outcomes or accredited. Making the choices and having some element of control often gives young people a major lift in self-esteem. Even if the decisions seem minor to us, they can be a radical new experience for those young people who are rarely consulted or have little control over their own lives.

- You will need to have buildings and contents insurance in place. You may have this in place as part of the policies of your local authority or voluntary organisation but in a small unit, you may have to arrange it yourself. The insurance schedule should be regularly updated for new equipment and specifically for expensive items such as cameras, audio–visual equipment or computers. It is not unknown in youth work circles for items to be stolen on arrival before workers have thought to insure them.

- Equipment needs to be regularly maintained, especially if it presents some sort of hazard such as electrical or outdoor pursuits equipment.

- Vehicles need servicing and testing. Running costs, vehicle checks and driver training will need an allocation in the budget. You will usually find that your local authority (often the education department) produces guidance on the use of minibuses and information is available on websites detailing the main regulations (for example The Scout Association, 2005; CPT, 2008).

- Your unit will need an inventory of equipment with serial numbers. This provides evidence for insurance purposes and for external funders. For sizeable group projects or capital grants, there should be agreements on what happens to equipment if the organisation or group folds. The inventory helps to ensure that resources do not simply get removed without authority.

- Equipment loans from partner agencies, sponsorship, or donations from local firms are all useful avenues to explore for resources. Some firms offer left over materials such as paper off-cuts or paint to community groups. Young people themselves can often make the most cogent case for support.

The 'small' resources are no different from all the other areas of the manager's responsibility. Systems are needed to avoid lurching from one unexpected crisis to another. More positively, management of both people and resources provides golden opportunities for welding a team together and developing young people's ability to take responsibility.

C H A P T E R   R E V I E W

This chapter starts from the premise that managing money and resources is an integral function for youth work and can be used proactively to help young people learn and develop. This raises the following issues.

- The need to be accountable and to know the extent of your own financial authority.

- Budgets should be set with the end users in mind. This means including the elements that will make the direct delivery to young people run smoothly. It also involves looking at service targets and gaps in provision and linking those processes effectively to budget setting.

- Finance should be transparent; you should be able to explain to your users how money is spent. To ensure that funds are effectively deployed, you will need a tight grip on the current position through regular monitoring.

- The management and maintenance of buildings can be a positive factor in making the facilities as welcoming to young people as possible.

- The manager is responsible for ensuring best practice in health and safety and safeguarding so that young people and their parents can be confident that they are protected from harm.

- All these processes and duties can be used to create opportunities for young people to learn and gain in skills and self-esteem.

FURTHER READING

Adirondack, S (2006) *Just about managing? Effective management for voluntary organisations and community groups*, 4th edition. London: London Voluntary Service Council.

Palmer, P (2005) *Financial management guide for the voluntary sector*. London: NCVO.

USEFUL WEBSITES

www.fmsis.info/index.asp Financial Management Standard in Schools

REFERENCES

Adirondack, S (2006) *Just about managing? Effective management for voluntary organisations and community groups*, 4th edition. London: London: London Voluntary Service Council.

Confederation of Passenger Transport UK (CPT) (2008) *Operating a minibus in the UK – brief guide.* Operational Briefing OP7.1. Online: **www.cpt-uk.org**

Field, R (2007) *Managing with plans and budgets in health and social care.* Exeter: Learning Matters.

Finance Hub (2008) *Managing money and resources.* Online: **www.financehub.org.uk/managing_money_and_resources/default/aspa**

Hackitt, J (2007) *Speech at the RSA Risk Commission conference.* October. Online: **www.hse.gov.uk/aboutus/speeches/pdfs/hackittrsa3110.htm** (accessed February 2008).

Health and Safety Executive (2003) *An introduction to health and safety.* INDG259 (rev). Sudbury: HSE Books. Online: **www.hse.gov.uk/pubns**

Health and Safety Executive (2006) *Five steps to risk assessment.* INDG163 (rev2). Sudbury: HSE Books.

NCVO (2007) *Introductory pack on funding and finance – guide to financial management.* **www.financehub.org.uk/uploads/documents/fh_guide_to_financial_management_May07_61.pdf**

NCVYS (2008) *Keeping it safe: a young person-centred approach to safety and child protection.* 2nd edition. London: NCVYS.

The Scout Association (2005) *General advice about running a minibus.* Online: **www.scoutbase.org.uk/library/misc/minibus.htm**

Chapter 6

Managing projects and programmes

Liz Hoggarth

Achieving your Youth and Community Work degree

This chapter is about developing the skills to bid for and manage short-term projects. It will help you to meet the following National Occupational Standards (February 2008).

- *4.2.3 Identify and address new youth work opportunities*

- *4.2.4 Identify and secure resources for youth work*

- *4.2.5 Work with providers of youth work activities*

- *4.2.6 Involve young people in the strategic development and delivery of the work*

- *4.2.7 Work in partnership with agencies to improve opportunities for young people*

- *4.4.1 Monitor and evaluate the quality of youth work activities*

Introduction

In this chapter, we explore the elements involved in managing projects. These usually fit within the wider youth work programme of your agency but they have separate funding for a defined purpose. They require the skills of bidding for the resources in the first place and then managing the progress of the work to ensure that staff are clear on their tasks, money is correctly spent and the targets are achieved on the required timescale. Since most funding bodies will now require evaluation, usually with evidence of the outcomes of the project, we also deal with the basic concepts of monitoring and evaluation. Managing projects can be a demoralising and negative experience if things start going wrong. It can also be fun and rewarding to see new developments come to fruition. So much money for work with young people is now made available for particular programmes (usually short term) that meet specific objectives. Unless you are prepared to miss out on those resources, you will need to develop these skills of project management.

A 'project' is usually taken to mean work with a particular purpose and a beginning and end date. Projects are time-limited, usually over a term of two to five years, and very often funded from external sources. In this context, the word 'programme' is used almost interchangeably but it can imply a series of interventions as part of the work such as in a 'training programme' or a 'research programme' to meet a particular need. Projects can be revenue projects using the funds for service provision or they can be capital projects using money for new buildings, improvements or new equipment or they can be a mix of both.

An effective youth worker will have established regular routes to find out information about new funding and commissioning. Although there is generally too much electronic and printed information to take in, there are some relevant and useful newsletters. For instance, Youth Policy Update from the National Youth Agency (NYA) is available free and the Strategic Information Service Bulletin from the National Council for Voluntary Youth Services (NCVYS) is available to its members. There may be more specific bulletins on local funding in your area. You need to work out which sources help you most and keep an ear to the ground in conversations with colleagues.

Before you even start applying for money or working up your project, however, you do need to be crystal clear about your reasons for wanting to do it. Workers and organisations can get into a tailspin by following every offer of external funding in an attempt just to survive or perhaps to expand their work. This can result in a loss of clarity of purpose and muddle about what the organisation stands for (often termed 'mission drift') and that does not help you in the long term. You should be able without any difficulty to show the relationship of your intended project to the targets your organisation has already set and if you cannot do that, it may be time to ask why you are bidding for this project.

You should also have a good look at the terms of the funding offer. If it has much too short a deadline to be realistic or a particular requirement (such as major matched funding from the private sector), then you may wish to give it a miss even if it fits with your own objectives. You should also consider the cost-benefit to your agency as, for example, a very small funding bid can sometimes take as much time and effort as a major scheme.

The big issues of project management

Whatever the shape and size of the project that you are contemplating, there are some critical factors you will always have to consider. Traditional project management theory sets out the constraints that face every project. These are sometimes expressed as the 'Project Management Triangle' of cost, scope and time (see, for instance, Microsoft Online, 2007 or the Project Smart website). How much money is available? What does the project have to achieve? What is the time frame?

The analogy is helpful because it enables you to identify what is given and unchangeable and therefore constrains the other 'sides' of the triangle. For example, if the funding available is finite and the period of a revenue project is fixed, then the only element of the plan you can really have control over is the number of young people you try to work with or how much you can do with them. If the project scope or requirements are inflexible and the end date is also fixed, you may need to budget for more staffing to achieve what is required in time.

The triangle picture still begs the question of the quality of the work. It is possible to find projects which have delivered the outputs they were supposed to achieve on time and without going over budget where people might nevertheless say that the project was not worthwhile or did not demonstrate really good practice. Some commentators therefore put quality at the centre of the triangle. You have choices to make about the quality of the work. Some of the practice will depend on your normal systems such as recruitment and training of skilled staff. Some factors depend on empathy, insight, commitment and attitude. Other elements must be built in, usually with a cost attached, to meet the needs of particular young people. For example, in work with young people who have achieved little in school, it may promote quality learning if there are two tutors so that more individual attention can be provided. In work with deaf young people, you might need staff with signing skills or extra computer support. In turn, the question of quality leads to the issue of the expectations of the users (the young people) and the funders and stakeholders. What is their view of the standard of provision they would wish or expect? Some authors have set this out as a 'project diamond' with expectations as a central theme (see Figure 6.1) (Haughey, 2008). These concepts are applicable to every project from a space launch to a youth festival. They may help you to think through your basic approach.

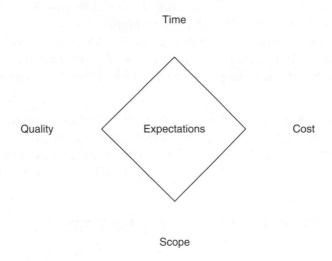

Figure 6.1 A project management 'diamond'

Bidding for the work

Understanding the requirements

The first step is to obtain a full copy of the requirements of the tender, commissioning process or funding scheme and the application form. Sometimes you will need to send in an Expression of Interest (EOI) to do this or complete a Pre-Qualification Questionnaire (PQQ) as a requirement to be allowed to apply especially in a commissioning process. These early processes simply establish that your organisation is suitable and sufficiently well managed to be capable of doing the work.

Once you have the requirements, read them with great care. Make sure you note the deadline, how many copies they need, any questions that will need a lot of work to answer, any items that will need the input of others and who will need to sign off the application. Writing a project bid is a project in itself – it involves planning and timing. Treat the outline of requirements like an exam question and ask yourself whether you have answered the question properly. Do not skip anything that is asked for and make sure all the 'boxes' are filled in. While this sounds foolishly obvious, you might be surprised how many bids fail simply because they do not supply the necessary information. Bids should look good, read well and be spell checked – it does not put your organisation in a good light if they are messy – ask someone to help you with presentation and writing skills if it is not your forte.

Information you need to show

Almost all project bids ask for similar elements. You can put yourself in a good position for bid writing by having some of these elements on file ready to be copied in or attached as appendices.

Most applications will ask you to show the following.

- A clear statement of what your organisation does and what its aims are, together with a brief description of its normal activities and how it is constituted. What is the 'mission' of the agency? Is it a local authority service, a voluntary organisation or another public or private service? Is it set up as a charity and/or a company limited by guarantee? You should have this prepared and approved by your board or managers as you will need it over and over again.

- Evidence for the need – what research have you done yourself about local need amongst young people? Is there evidence from other studies or statistical sources that confirms that need? Is there a business plan or feasibility study? Keep references to research you have seen on relevant topics and use the local authority websites and other agencies for local statistics.

- A description of the project you propose – this needs to include the aims of the project, what groups of young people it will work with, its activities and methods and how it will be managed. This should not be wrapped up in jargon. Ask yourself 'What will the project actually do?' and describe it simply.

- Evidence that your organisation is competent to carry out the work – this involves checking that you have the necessary infrastructure in place and having the records or documents to prove it. We develop this theme further on to show what you need to have in place and on file.

- A realistic and well-thought-out budget – you should include all the resources you need to deliver the project properly. Chapter 5 shows an example of drawing up a project budget. Do include a figure for evaluation as projects will normally need to produce evidence of results. A specific financial analysis may be required such as the breakdown into each year of the project or into particular headings. Remember also that it is legitimate for a voluntary organisation to include overheads such as the cost of the time spent by managers in supervising the project or administrative support from your organisation. You can usually get guidance from funders on the percentage of overheads they will allow in a bid. Although it is working through slowly, this principle of 'full cost recovery' was accepted by the Treasury in 2002 (DCSF, 2007) and helpful guidance is now available to voluntary organisations (ACEVO, 2007).

- A timetable with key events or 'milestones' to get the project delivered – what will you need in place by when if the project is to achieve its goals in time? This might, for example, include planning permission for an extension or recruitment of new staff to deliver the project.

- The outputs and outcomes the project will achieve; you need to be able to distinguish between outputs and outcomes for your project and set them out clearly (see the section on evaluation below and more about outputs and outcomes in Chapter 7). Most funders are most interested in the outcomes or benefits to the users. Will anybody be better off as a result of this project? There are skills involved in setting project outcome targets and these are discussed in more detail below. You may also need to detail how the outcomes you set will contribute to the targets set by the funder or for local strategies and targets such as those in Local Area Agreements or regeneration schemes.

- Proposals for how you will monitor and evaluate the project. Here 'monitoring' refers to producing regular project data such as figures for attendance and to the checking of progress on a continuing basis. 'Evaluation' refers to the assessment of the effectiveness of the project in particular what outcomes it achieved. Your planning for monitoring and evaluation is a critical area of project work and is developed more fully below.

Depending on the specific funding scheme, other details may also be required such as an estimate of risks and contingencies, the partners involved and so on. There is helpful guidance available to voluntary organisations from NCVO and other bodies on fundraising and dealing with service level agreements, contracts and tenders (e.g. NCVO, 2007; Whiter, 2006) and most of the information readily transfers to local authority youth work units, which may also be bidding for additional funding. Chapter 7 looks at tenders and commissioning.

Setting up infrastructures

You can place yourself in an optimum position to make successful bids by making sure that you have the basic infrastructure in place. That means the systems and procedures that support an organisation rather than its constitutional framework. Funders and commissioners ask about these things because they want to make sure they are dealing with a reputable organisation that is really capable of managing and delivering a project. If your organisation cannot produce the items listed below, then it is well worth your while investing time in developing the basics to begin with rather than rushing to make funding bids immediately. It looks a long list but the effort to prepare will pay huge dividends to the speed and credibility of your responses to calls for new projects. There is never any guarantee that some funder will not ask for something else (and some already do) but if these things are readily available, anything else should be fairly easy to produce.

Necessary systems and procedures

Typically you will need to have available and readily accessible on file the following items:

- audited accounts for the previous financial year;
- your constitution (for a voluntary organisation) or a description of your organisation's place in a local authority structure;
- records (if your agency is a company) of the company registration number, the date on which it was established and names of company directors;
- details of any charitable status and charity number;
- a list of the Management Committee, Board members or Trustees together with any conflicts of interest such as Board members related to councillors on the local authority;
- records of insurance and copies of policies for public liability, employer's liability and any professional indemnity;
- the numbers of staff and a structure chart;
- a staff development and training policy;
- a health and safety policy;
- a child protection/safeguarding policy and procedures;
- a risk assessment procedure;
- an accident recording system and previous accident statistics;
- a complaints procedure;
- an equal opportunities policy including equalities policies in relation to user access and to the recruitment and training of staff;
- evidence of Criminal Records Bureau checks in place for staff working directly with young people;
- any quality assurance programmes the agency has completed/is working on such as PQASSO, Investors in People or ISO9001:2000 and the level you have achieved;
- details of previous projects or contracts and preferably the names and contact details of people who have agreed to be contacted for a reference on the quality of the work;
- for some charitable organisations, a financial risk assessment policy dealing with the policy on reserves and other matters of financial management.

Clarifying tasks and deadlines

A sense of timing is critical for successful project work. This applies to the job of getting the bid finished and submitted on time and needs to be considered in relation to delivering the project in reality if you are successful. You often need to put the 'milestones' into the proposal but you will need more detail for your own purposes to remind you and other staff about what has to be done. For instance, to have new staff in place to start the project you will probably need to advertise, interview and induct them before you can begin to deliver or if the time frame is very short you may need temporary staff to get things going. Similarly in order to start activities, all the risk assessments will need to be completed and Criminal Records Bureau checks may be needed for new staff. Essentially these steps are no different from the tasks involved in everyday management of staff and resources outlined in Chapters 4 and 5 but there will often be added pressures in project work to see delivery happening quickly to meet the targets set.

A good tip is to take the date at which the project money must be spent up and claimed. Then work backwards to list each step that must be taken to ensure that happens. If you show who is responsible for each step, this makes the basis of a practical work plan. This may seem somewhat obsessive but will in fact pay dividends. It will give you something against which to check progress with sufficient detail to make sure vital links are not over-looked. Remember that some funding bodies reclaim their money if it is not spent in time or the targets are not achieved.

Above all the jobs and their deadlines need to be communicated to the staff who will have to complete the work. Clear communication is crucial and that includes the purpose of the project, its criteria and constraints and all the tasks that will be required. Remember that if project teams wander from the agreed purpose of the project or get too far behind on timescales, funders may suspend or withdraw funding. Do not forget that all your current staff also need to be aware of the project and where it fits with the whole organisation and ideally they should be able to contribute to the planning and creative thinking involved in its preparation.

There are countless project management tools available. It seems as if a new one is invented by a management guru somewhere almost every week. Many can be viewed or downloaded free from the web (just search on 'project management'). You do not in fact need any complex tools to manage typical youth work projects so long as you keep a grip on the basic elements of time, cost and scope discussed above. Some tools are commonly used in major projects and can be helpful such as the Gantt chart, which can be created on Excel or a similar spreadsheet to show the time line for the whole project and the timing needed for each particular activity. You can also draw your own Critical Path Analysis, which is simply a diagram or flow chart which shows what tasks have to be done and where they must be done in parallel (for illustrations see the Businessballs website).

Creating and leading the team

The principles of managing project staff are in essence no different from those of managing permanent staff in ongoing work. The principal elements such as good recruitment, induction and training have already been described in Chapter 4. The main difference in relation to project teams is that they are set up on a short-term basis to achieve delivery of a particular piece of work. Everything has to be telescoped down into a shorter period if the end result is to be reached in time. This means you have to put things in place faster. For instance, if you are starting a mountain biking project and training on health and safety procedures is required for the new workers, you should ideally have the training provider and the dates fixed up early on so that new staff can complete it before they have to be out working with young people. Time may need to be built in for team building and briefings to speed up the coherence, sense of purpose and mutual support in the team. It may be that with the possibilities of transfer, secondment or acting up, not all the project team will be new staff. Some may even contribute to more than one project team. The key principles remain the same – everybody needs to be clear about the objectives of the project and to be well prepared for their role in the team.

There can be effects from other differences. Project workers will sometimes have a greater need for support because of the timescales, and because the target groups are often young people at risk. The teams will go through the normal stages of group formation but you need to pay close attention to any serious conflicts developing within the team or failures to support each other and resolve them as quickly as possible. Project teams sometimes see themselves as separate from the 'mainstream' staff or they may feel some special status from the 'innovative' nature of the project. The senior manager needs to guard against divisions within the agency or failure of project staff to refer appropriately or to see corporate procedures as necessary and applicable. Everybody contributes to the overall effort of youth work even if some people work in 'special' projects. There will also inevitably be an effect at the end of the project from the fixed-term contracts. Unless you can secure continuation at least six months before the project ends, or guarantee a suitable job somewhere else in the organisation, people will start to look for new jobs and you may need to put in extra resources to make sure that the project is properly concluded.

Mann (2002) has argued that project teams are becoming more common as organisations become leaner and resources are more limited. He suggests that for maximum effectiveness, project teams require clarity at the outset, training and skill development, a supportive culture, maintenance of good working relationships and clear communication.

Sorting the resources

In Chapter 5, the main strands of good resource management have been outlined. Projects also need to follow these basic principles of planning and managing a budget. If there are differences from 'mainstream' finances, they lie mainly in the short-term nature of most project funding and with the targeting of particular needs.

From the start you should be clear about the requirements of the funder and the final and interim deadlines for financial reporting. Communicate that timetable to the key people. Project staff may need to know when expense claims or orders must be completed. Administrative staff may have to submit grant claims or invoices. Codes should be set up early on so that there is no delay to spend and project codes should reflect the separate funding source. As noted in Chapter 5, you should never be tempted to use project monies as a temporary fix for your mainstream budget problems.

Most projects will be created because there is a gap in provision, a group with particular needs or an area with features of deprivation or low achievement. It follows that the project resources need to be tailored to make sure of the best possible chance of meeting those needs. Project staff need to know how much freedom they have to make decisions and what flexibility they have to incur expenditure to deal with issues faced by the young people. For example, research on youth engagement has repeatedly shown that for young people to volunteer or to be able to engage properly with a youth forum or some other democratic structure, most will need some help with transport or expenses, especially those who are most vulnerable (Low and Butt, 2007; Skinner and Fleming, 2007). To cope with this a participation project would need a designated allocation for transport, travel expenses or passes and a clear system for authorising and claiming the spend.

ACTIVITY **6.1**

A project funded by the Teenage Pregnancy Strategy sets out to train young parents and involve them in offering a peer education programme to pupils in Year 11 at local schools. Are there any particular elements you would build into the project budget to be sure that the young parents can play their part fully and achieve what is intended?

Can you give examples from your own practice of situations where flexible resources have been needed to ensure effective project work with particular groups of young people?

Following through and managing the glitches

Keeping in touch

It is not uncommon for project staff to have virtually no contact from their senior manager until the deadline for the quarterly report makes for a sudden urgent memo. Needless to say that is hardly good practice. The senior manager faces two ways, both ensuring that the funder's requirements are met and that problems are solved with the delivery staff.

In relation to the funding body, it is important to keep in touch and make a relationship of trust with their responsible project officer. If major problems are occurring, achievement of targets is slow or spend is not working out as expected, it is normally best to inform the funder. There may be some flexibility that can be allowed and above all you want to avoid 'claw back' of the money. Conversely they also need the good news; the reassurance that what they have funded is producing a positive effect, and may indeed be more helpful with the problem situations if they believe the project is doing good work.

Solving problems

The first approach to problems is to try to anticipate them. In 'management speak', this is called 'managing risks and contingencies'. It involves thinking about what is most likely to delay or inhibit the project and sometimes you will need to indicate these issues in your bid. Ask yourself the 'what if' questions. If your project needs to reach young people with disabilities and you hope to do that through their schools, what if the strategy does not work? How would you adapt your approach to try another avenue? 'What if' nobody answers the advertisement for staff? Is there any other way of running the project? This thought process will in fact help you to avoid the worst pitfalls and to have a fall-back position if they do occur.

The second tactic is obviously to catch the problems early and sort out them out: no challenging project will run entirely smoothly. As we have seen in earlier chapters, good routines of staff supervision help you to see the problems as they arise and to co-operate with your workers in finding solutions. The need to solve problems obviously does not lie exclusively in project work but it is imperative in short-term projects that the particular demands of the work are thought through and that any snags are addressed quickly.

There are numerous sources of advice and models of problem solving in books and on websites (e.g. **www.businessballs.com** or **www.managementhelp.org**). Although many of them refer most closely to the commercial world, they can be useful in giving you pointers to the questions you are avoiding or the steps you have skipped. Leaving aside specific models for analysing problem issues, the basic steps of problem solving are often outlined as follows (see Businessballs, 2009).

- *Clarify in your own mind exactly what you think the problem is*. It may not be what people say first, the 'presenting problem'. Decide whether it is a trivial problem or one that really will influence the success or failure of the project.

- *Gather the facts and decide what is causing it*. Keep asking 'why'. Maybe your project has not recruited enough new minority ethnic young people to meet its targets. Why? Because the staff decided to recruit by advertising in the local press. Why? Because that was all they could think of, as they have little awareness of either minority group networks, the minority press or where young people read or listen to information. Why? Because they have had little experience and no awareness training. Why? Because you did not manage to fix it up for their induction and the project had to start. Why? Because you did not plan sufficiently well in advance.

- *Think broadly and list all the possible options and solutions you come up with*. Unless the problem is around staff relationships or performance, you will probably want to consult your team and involve them in contributing possible ways forward.

- *List the pros and cons of the options*. This can be a simple list but there are more elaborate ways of scoring options. Remember to include the feelings that you and others will have about the potential solutions: emotional resistance, fears or reservations can stop a perfectly rational option from working if they are not taken into account.

- *Choose the option that seems most likely to work*. Try to avoid compromise options: you will rarely be able to please everybody.

- *Explain your choice to those who will be affected and will have to implement it*. If people can see the reasoning behind the decision, they may be more inclined to try to make it work than if it is imposed without explanation. Remember that even an imperfect decision is better than paralysis or dithering; at least you are trying a way forward.

- *Follow up on your chosen course of action*. You need to ensure that staff are putting the plan into practice and then to check if the 'solution' is in fact working. If it is not, you have to think again.

Some project teams get bogged down in the problems and dwell too much on how challenging it all is. It is worth pausing a moment to reflect on the strand of thinking about problem solving known as 'appreciate inquiry' (Hammond, 1998). Instead of using traditional problem solving to analyse the issue and the solutions, this approach starts from appreciating what works well and what is worth building on. Differences are valued. From there a team can picture 'what might be' and make new plans on how to get there. If negativity is setting in, the manager could do worse than draw on these insights to encourage and value what people do best.

Monitoring, evaluation and reporting

Virtually all projects and special programmes require some form of reporting back to the funding body and possibly also to steering committees or other such support structures. A great many projects fall down or are even suspended because they fail to think through what is needed and set up monitoring and evaluation systems from the beginning. In the discussion of bid writing above, we defined 'monitoring' as the gathering of regular project data and the ongoing checking of progress. There will frequently be requirements for such figures on a quarterly basis. We defined 'evaluation' as the assessment of the effectiveness of the project, in particular what outcomes it achieved. Such reports are normally required annually and/or at the end of your project.

Outputs and outcomes – understanding the main terms

Government strategy for children and young people has moved over the last five to ten years to focus on outcomes. From *Youth Matters* to the *Ten Year Strategy for Young People* (DfES, 2005; DCSF, 2007) the concept of outcomes keeps coming through. National guidance to services for children and young people now demands that they start commissioning to achieve the targets of *Every Child Matters* (DfES, 2006) (see Chapter 7). Simply offering the same provision over and over will not suffice. Government, public services and charities want to know that what they fund does make a difference. If you can show that you understand this context in your bids and can then evidence that your project has achieved results and delivered on its intended outcomes, you will gain real credibility in this competitive arena.

First you do need to understand the jargon.

- An *outcome* can be defined (Kellogg Foundation, 2004, p2) as the 'specific changes in program participants' behaviour, knowledge, skills, status and level of functioning'. Friedman offers a simpler formula: 'a result (or outcome or goal) is a population condition of wellbeing for children, adults, families and communities, stated in plain language' (Friedman, 2005, p19). In other words, outcomes look at the difference our provision makes to the individual young person and to young people in our community as a whole.

- *Activities* are what we do to achieve that change, such as providing counselling, or drama groups or volunteering opportunities. Projects will be offering very different activities depending on their aims and their specialisms.

- *Outputs* are the tangible products of the project, such as the numbers attending or the numbers of health packs distributed. They are counted to describe and quantify the size of the programme. That applies both to activities (how many basketball coaching sessions were offered) and to participants (who was reached, how many people came to the sessions).

- *Inputs* are the things that go in to make the programme work, including money, time, workers, vehicles and facilities.

- *Indicators* are the things you collect and measure to help you decide if the outcome has been achieved. It is often not possible to measure an outcome directly: indicators work as proxy for what you need to know about. For example, you will not be able to measure how many young people are using illegal drugs because people are understandably reticent about such behaviour. If you are running a drug prevention project, you might, however, choose indicators about how many young people say they are now more aware of the dangers, or how many are attending and completing treatment.

- *Impact* is 'the effect of a project at a higher or broader level, in the longer term, after a range of outcomes has been achieved' (Cupitt and Ellis, 2007, p6). The terms 'outcomes' and 'impact' are sometimes used interchangeably to denote the effects that programmes have. Generally it is helpful to think of impact as longer term.

There is more information about these terms in Chapter 7 in relation to managing performance. Different models use these terms in slightly different ways. Remember that strictly speaking 'outcomes' can be negative too. A sarcastic youth worker who undermines the efforts of the young people will not help them develop and may leave them worse off. The broader definition of outcomes as 'the changes, benefits, learning and other effects that happen as a result of your work' (Cupitt and Ellis, 2007, p6) may be more accurate. The essential point, however, is to make the distinction between the resources you put in, the activities and outputs you deliver and the effect of all that effort on your participants. The central questions are 'What difference does it make?' and 'How can I show evidence of that change?'

Logic models are commonly used to assist planning for projects and social programmes (see **www.healthscotland.com/understanding/evaluation/support/logic-models.aspx** and Penna and Phillips, 2005). The principle of logic modelling is that you decide what you want to achieve, the state of affairs you want to create and then you specify the chain of steps that will lead to that situation. In other words you start with the outcome you want to see and decide what you and others involved have to do to get there. It is then possible to evaluate whether the outcome was achieved or not and to examine the links in the chain to see what happened. There are many forms of these models, often described under other names such as programme theory, theory-based evaluation or results accountability, each with a slightly different emphasis and its own terminology. You need to be aware that many commissioners are using this way of planning services and deciding what they will fund. The approach can also help you to decide with young people what they want to achieve and how to get there.

Apply the hypothetical example below to a project you know well. Can you express its outcomes clearly and simply? Use the matrix below to list its outputs and how they are monitored. Then list the outcomes and suggest the indicators you might choose and how you would collect the evidence for them.

Table 6.1 Hypothetical project

Project name: *Signpost Youth Advice Line*

Purpose: To provide telephone advice and signposting for young people

Activities **(focus of the work)**

Free phone line and website enquiries; advice and information for young people by trained telephone advisers.

Outputs	How are they monitored?	Outcomes (benefits for the users – the effect of the work)	Indicators (what will show the outcome has been achieved?)	How will the evidence be collected?
Number of days and hours per annum line operated	Admin staff record any closures against expected operating days	Young people know where to go for positive activities	Number of queries answered on activities	Adviser records query and answer. Data collated by administrator
Number of callers (with age, ethnicity and gender)	Adviser makes computer record and asks for age and ethnicity with type of query	Young people feel better informed on health risks	Number of queries answered on health matters	As above
Number of hits on website	Admin staff collate call records and web hits		Opinions of users	
Number of referrals to other services	Adviser records referral on computer system	Young people are satisfied with service and more confident to make decisions for themselves		Telephone survey to check satisfaction and ask key questions on gains in awareness and confidence

Essential steps to effective evaluation and monitoring

Whatever the nature of your project, the critical questions that you need to answer remain the same. Use the resources available from national agencies. The Charities Evaluation Service, for instance, offers help through its own publications and links to other references (CES, 2005). Plan your evaluation effort early and build it into everyday work. Use this sequence of questions for your planning.

- What is the project setting out to change?

- What are the project's activities to achieve that change?

- What are the project outputs? What information do the funders want to see about them and when?

- What output information do you therefore need to collect? Who is responsible for doing it?

- What are the intended outcomes of the project? (You should state them simply and in a way that an ordinary person in the street would understand.)

- What indicators will you use to show the evidence of those outcomes? (Take just two or three measures for an outcome; you cannot collect everything.)

- What methods could you use to collect the data on those indicators?

- So what will you actually collect as evidence of the outcomes?

- Who will collect the data (surveys, interview notes, etc.)?

- Who will analyse it and write it up?

- When is the evaluation report needed?

- Will you need external support to complete evaluation requirements? (You need to budget for staff time and/or external consultancy or research support.)

Friedman suggests that effective evaluation will offer four essential perspectives on a service or project. These questions are set out in Table 6.2, which is adapted from Friedman's work and tailored to the youth work context. It can be used to review how your project is performing or to judge whether you are collecting adequate evidence for evaluation purposes. 'Is anyone better off?' is the question which addresses outcomes. This is the most important question and ideally the answer to that should provide both qualitative and quantitative evidence.

Data collection and analysis

Monitoring and evaluation should be embedded in everyday project activity. It can be a natural and fun part of the activities with young people if properly planned (Comfort et al., 2006). It will all be a lot less painful if the right information is gathered from the very beginning and if all staff understand their part in collecting or entering the data. Information input should happen regularly: much good evidence is lost because nobody collated attendance figures, evaluation forms or questionnaires at the time. If

Table 6.2 Questions for effective evaluation

How much did the project do?	How well did it do it?
For example, evidence of: • number of young people attending • number of sessions held • number of outreach contacts made • total actual expenditure for the year	For example, evidence of: • reach in terms of ethnicity, gender, disability • satisfaction of the users • cost per activity session/young person • young people's participation • compliance with reporting requirements

Is anyone better off?

Qualitative	*Quantitative*
For example, evidence of: • detail of successful outcomes, changes young people have made • quotations from interviews with young people • case studies • evidence from parents or carers	Evidence of the proportion or percentage of those who reported successful outcomes (were 'better off'). For example: • percentage gaining accreditation • proportion reporting increased self-confidence • percentage with increased school attendance • number of young people entering jobs or training (no longer NEET)

questionnaires or databases are to be used, they should be piloted first to ensure they work effectively. Data can be quantitative (numbers, proportions, etc.) or qualitative (material which tells the story, gives the feel of what happened and people's perceptions). It is important to gather both.

Your role as project manager in communicating what needs to be done is central. In many projects, the team is not even fully aware of the outcomes they are supposed to be achieving let alone how those are evaluated. In one youth project, for instance, a careful design was prepared of 'before' and 'after' questions to the young people about what they had gained from their participation. The part-time staff administered the right questions at the beginning of the project work but forgot to use the 'after' questions at the end, thus wasting all the effort. They had never understood how important it was to collect the evidence of progress or the part they had to play in it.

You should be analysing what you collect as you go along but do allow sufficient time for writing up the analysis and polishing your report. Data analysis is concerned with organising the evidence in a logical way and drawing out the main patterns it shows. Remember that the main task is to provide evidence of your outcomes. Think about the words, ideas or events you are looking for – your indicators. What categories can you put them into? What are the extremes, the highs and lows in the data? Quantitative data can be analysed statistically, showing, for example, percentages, averages, trends or the range of responses. Someone within the project needs to be familiar with software such as Excel and able to present findings efficiently in charts and figures. If you do not have that capacity, you will need to find it externally. Qualitative information is often harder to analyse and it helps to have a clear idea of the indicators you are looking for. Are there themes you can use to show the connections and patterns? Look for examples and quotations in your qualitative material that can illustrate and enliven your report. Use a simple coding system or a highlighter pen to identify related points, or you can 'cut and paste' to put data under specific themes. Make sure that you do not ignore the contrary points or negative comments, as you need to address these rather than simply use what favours the project.

The best advice is to take advice before you finalise your plans for data collection. Even if you do not employ an external evaluator, you should be able to find a researcher or a student who can help you. It may be possible to ask someone to design the evaluation methods for you and then write it up after your project team have collected the data itself. To obtain statistically valid results (if you need and want to do so) requires a representative and sufficiently large sample.

Be wary of two extremes that are frequently seen in project reports. The first is to claim a causal link – that the project interventions caused the change – when this cannot be supported with statistical validity. Few typical youth work projects will have the know-how or resources to complete studies which validly show cause and effect. Usually the most you can say is that the evidence on the indicators supports the view that the project has contributed to the change, generally along with the efforts of other partners. It is better to say that than make nonsense claims. The other extreme is to depend on one or two qualitative case studies. While a good example does enliven a report, one endearing story does not provide evidence of overall effectiveness.

The quality of your monitoring and evaluation is a crucial element in your overall project management. It is worth taking it seriously and embedding it in the life of the project from the start. It can bring real credibility and help to secure future funding either for the individual project or for your agency as a whole.

Reputation and credibility

You need to pay attention at each stage to the image of your project. We have tried to show throughout this book that as a youth worker you have to face towards different audiences simultaneously. In project work, you must gain respect from the young people and the community in which you operate. You will also face your funding body and their demands. Your project could conceivably make an impact on wider youth work policy as well or the provision for young people in your local area.

Projects need to be well publicised with their target group in ways that speak of their relevance and capacity to relate well to young people. Once your users have 'come through the door', your work will be shrewdly assessed. Young people will rate you and your team for doing what you promise, trustworthiness, their enjoyment and the gains they make through participation. Reputation goes round like wildfire, which is the reason why the most effective recruitment to youth projects is often by word of mouth. Despite the pressures of short timescales, be careful not to offer false promises of immediate gains. Young people frequently report their disappointment about how long real change can take for themselves or for their community: it is better to be realistic at the outset.

Older people in the community or other agencies may also need convincing, especially if the project challenges cultural patterns or existing agency provision or reaches vulnerable or antisocial young people. If 'rewards' are offered, ensure that your messages show clearly that they are a response to achievement and that there are boundaries for behaviour in the project. Team members need to present themselves professionally in these contexts, however informal the approach may be inside the project itself.

You may have opportunities for wider influence, especially if your project can demonstrate successful outcomes. Some projects are linked to others in wider programmes; some funding bodies want to profile their best work. There may be opportunities to publicise positive images of young people, contribute to websites or to use evaluation findings strategically. Take these chances as much as your time will allow – much inspirational project work never sees the light of day in terms of the wider world. People who know how to reach young people and how the barriers they face can be surmounted need to have a voice when policy is made. Remember, however, to use your skills of networking and collaboration and to give due credit to your partners (partnership and networking are discussed in Chapter 7). There are few issues now not influenced by partnership structures as working together has been so much emphasised in the face of complex problems. Even if you run a brilliant project, a 'prima donna' attitude will not increase your sphere of influence (see Chapter 8 on increasing it).

C H A P T E R   R E V I E W

This chapter does not stand alone. Project management involves all the key principles of managing yourself, your staff and your resources as covered in previous chapters. It emphasises that such issues are made more acute by the short-term nature and specific targets of most projects. It has explored:

- the constraints on projects of cost, scope and time and the need to factor in the expectations of users and funders;

- how to put yourself in the best position of readiness for bidding for funds by preparing your essential documentation and setting up the necessary infrastructure and procedures;

- dealing with the time pressures of project work;

- leading the team and sorting out the problems which arise;

- the importance of monitoring and evaluation and the essential steps involved in collecting evidence for your outcomes;

- the need to build and guard the reputation and credibility of your project and take opportunities to influence wider policy making.

Charities Evaluation Service (2005) *Practical monitoring and evaluation – a guide for voluntary organisations.* 2nd edition. London: Charities Evaluation Service.

Hoggarth, L and Comfort, H (2010 forthcoming) *A practical guide to outcome evaluation.* London: Jessica Kingsley.

Lawrie, A (2006) *The complete guide to creating and managing new projects for voluntary organisations.* 2nd edition. London: Directory of Social Change.

ACEVO www.ncvo-vol.org.uk/sfp/?id=2111

www.financehub.org.uk/uploads/documents/fh_guide_to_fundraising_May07_48.pdf

www.hm-treasury.gov.uk/media/2/6/cyp_tenyearstrategy_260707.pdf

ACEVO and New Philanthropy Capital (2007) *Guide to full cost recovery.* London: ACEVO. Online: **www.ncvo-vol.org.uk/sfp/?id=2111**

Businessballs (2008) *Project management – tools, process, plans and project planning tips.* Online: **www.businessballs.com/project.htm**

Businessballs (2009) *Problem-solving and decision-making.* Online: **www.businessballs.com/problemsolving.htm**

Charities Evaluation Service (2005) *Practical monitoring and evaluation – a guide for voluntary organisations*, 2nd edition. London: Charities Evaluation Service.

Comfort, H with Merton, B, Payne, M and Flint, W (2006) *Capturing the evidence – tools and processes for recognising and recording the impact of youth work.* Leicester: National Youth Agency.

Cupitt, S and Ellis, J (2007) *Your project and its outcomes.* London: Charities Evaluation Service. Online: **www.ces-vol.org.uk/downloads/yourprojectanditsoutcomes-139-146.pdf**

Department for Children, Schools and Families (2007) *Aiming high: ten year strategy for young people.* Online: **http://publications.dcsf.gov.uk/eOrderingDownload/PU214.pdf**

Department for Education and Skills (2005) *Youth matters,* Cm 6629, London: DfES.

Department for Education and Skills (2006) *Every child matters.* London: DfES.

Department for Education and Skills (2006) *Joint planning and commissioning framework for children, young people and maternity services.* London: DfES. Online: **www.everychildmatters.gov.uk**

Friedman, M (2005) *Trying hard is not good enough: how to produce measurable improvements for customers and communities.* Victoria, Canada: Trafford Publishing.

Hammond, SA (1998) *The thin book of appreciative inquiry,* 2nd edition. Bend, Oregon: Thin Book Publishing Company.

Haughey, D (2008) *An introduction to project management.* Online: **www.projectsmart.co.uk/introduction-to-project-management.html**

WK Kellogg Foundation (2004) *Logic model development guide.* Michigan: WK Kellogg Foundation. Online: **www.wkkf.org/Pubs/Tools/Evaluation/Pub3669.pdf**

Low, N and Butt, S (2007) *Helping out: a national survey of volunteering and charitable giving.* London: National Centre for Social Research and the Institute for Volunteering Research.

Mann, S (2002) 'Working around projects', *Professional manager,* November, 29–32.

Microsoft Online (2007) *Every project plan is a triangle.* Online: **http://office.microsoft.com**

NCVO/Institute of Fundraising (2007) *Introductory pack on funding and finance – guide to fundraising.* Online: **www.financehub.org.uk/uploads/documents/fh_guide_to_fundraising_May07_48.pdf**

Penna, R and Phillips, W (2005) 'Eight outcome models', *Evaluation exchange, X1,* 2. Harvard Family Research Project. Online: **www.hfrp.org/evaluation/the-evaluation-exchange/issue-archive/evaluation-methodology/eight-outcome-models**

Skinner, A and Fleming, J (2007*) Influence through participation.* London: IDeA.

Whiter, R (2006) *Before signing on the dotted line: all you need to know about procuring public sector contracts.* London: National Council for Voluntary Organisations. Online: **www.ncvo-vol.org.uk**

Chapter 7

Managing a public service in a business culture

Bryan Merton

Achieving your Youth and Community Work degree

This chapter is about policy change, commissioning, collaborative working, performance management and innovation. It will help you to meet the following National Occupational Standards (February 2008).

- *3.3.2 Develop productive relationships with colleagues and stakeholders*

- *4.2.3 Identify and address new youth work opportunities*

- *4.2.7 Work in partnership with agencies to improve opportunities for young people*

- *4.4.1 Monitor and evaluate the quality of youth work activities*

Introduction

In this chapter we explain how the changes in public policy over the last 30 years have affected services for young people, including youth work. We show how attempts to introduce a market into public services are leading to a commissioning process designed to clarify expectations, specify requirements and bring into play a wider range of service suppliers. We set out what this means for youth workers and their skills in management, including how they manage their performance. We show that managing services for young people in the current policy climate requires youth workers to analyse the interests of stakeholders, develop partnerships with other service suppliers and create networks so that the expectations of all stakeholders for efficient and effective provision can be met. We stress the importance of innovation if youth work is to remain dynamic and responsive; and the importance of demonstrating that the work that is done with young people is of public value.

Making the policy shift

Over the last 30 years there has been a major change in the ways in which public services have been perceived, managed and provided. These contrast sharply with the dominant culture of the first 30 years of the welfare state. In the first period (1948–78) public services were seen as the province of the state – both national government and local authorities. The health service, schools, transport, the major utilities and industries such as coal, gas and steel were seen as properly being in public ownership. Under Conservative and successive New Labour governments over the second period (1979–2009), the policy has been to introduce efficiencies by privatising the major industries and transport and by introducing more of a market to public services and opening them up to the private sector and to what is now known as the third sector – voluntary and community organisations and social enterprises. The premise upon which this policy is based is that services will become more efficient if the previous monopoly provision by the state is broken up and 'customers' are offered greater choice and diversity. It is a policy that is much contested both by service users and those who provide the services.

Many people working in these services do so because they are committed to the idea of being in public service. The assumption is that we pay taxes to join society in the same way that we pay a 'membership fee' in return for which we expect to receive certain benefits, goods and services free or at very modest cost. Government policy has been to shift the role of the state from being the single provider of such services to being the commissioner by securing services from other suppliers.

ACTIVITY **7.1**

- *What do you think of this shift in policy?*

- *Is it one to which you subscribe?*

- *Would you rather see the state as the single provider?*

- *When thinking about this you need to consider which model of public service provision works in the best interests of young people; what evidence do you have to support your point of view?*

Creating a market

The business model has prevailed and public services, including youth work, are increasingly being put out to tender. Local authorities are no longer expected to provide services directly themselves but to secure them and ensure what is referred to as 'contestability'. As far as youth work is concerned, or more specifically the positive activities which form a core component of the youth offer (this will be discussed more fully later in this chapter), government expects there to be a market at which providers from different sectors can display their wares and from which young people can choose which activities or programmes they want to take part in.

There are two sets of reasons for introducing markets to public services, *managerial* and *political*. The *managerial* rationale concerns efficiency for which two different arguments are proposed. The first is *productive* efficiency where goods and services are provided at lower costs and the low-cost providers will replace the high-cost providers; this is said to encourage new entrants to come to the market. Second, there is *allocative* efficiency where only goods and services that people demand will enter the market (Flynn 2007, p 203). The rationale is that the response of providers to the demands of users is more likely to produce what people want than some bureaucratic procedure. If these efficiency aspects are to prevail, the service user has to know what is available and how to access it. Service providers, such as youth workers, have to ensure that the user has access to the relevant information and may have to stimulate demand too.

The second reason is *political* in the sense that when it comes to public services politicians, whether they be national or local, do not like to be seen to be closing things down unless they are dangerously or dishonestly run. No councillor is likely to propose the closure of a local amenity if there is some evidence that the local community wants it to stay. However, if the market forces closure, then the politician is off the hook.

So for reasons of efficiency and politics markets have been introduced by policy makers, often under the guise of giving people greater choice and control over public services. There has been some ideological spice added to the policy as well. Compulsory competitive tendering was first introduced under a Thatcher Conservative government in order to break up the monopoly control exercised by local authorities and to give the private sector greater business opportunities (Flynn, 2007).

So for a number of reasons features of the public service landscape have been opened up to the market place. Commissioning, which is perhaps a less politically charged term than compulsory competitive tendering, is the process through which this is done.

In its guidance to local authorities on their duty to secure positive activities the government is specific:

> *The local authority . . . should seek to manage its resources as efficiently as possible. It should use the service provider that offers the best possible combination of skills and experience to deliver services of the highest possible quality and for the most economical cost.*
> (Para 79)

> *[When considering alternative provision to its own the local authority should] consult other 'persons' it considers appropriate . . . partner agencies, professional organisations or other independent bodies and individuals operating in an advisory capacity.*
> (Para 82)

> *[The local authority should] satisfy itself that it has assessed the merits of different delivery options . . . and will also need to provide alternative providers with the information they need to decide whether to take an interest.*
> (Para 83)

> *The criteria for considering which provider to secure services from include:*

> * *cost to the service user and to the authority;*

> * *quality;*

- *timing;*

- *location;*

- *access to target groups and individuals;*

- *sustainability;*

- *and whether an alternative provider would be better placed to respond to young people's needs/desires.*
(Para 86)

Local authorities should identify clearly the outcomes sought before commissioning positive activities. They should also recognise that service level agreements can provide a helpful way to record expectations of quality and performance – [i.e. what is to be done and how well it should be done].
(Para 89)

(DCSF, 2008)

How does this impact on youth workers? Whether you work for the local authority or for a voluntary organisation it requires you to be able to demonstrate that the provision you make is efficient, effective and produces the outcomes required. If the project or centre you work in is to be considered for commissioning, it has to be noticed and on the database that local authorities and their partners are now required to have in place (on the internet) so that young people know what kinds of positive activities are available, where, at what times, at what price and of what quality. Never has it been more important for youth work projects to promote their projects and have supporting evidence to show that the work is good and worth investing in. Youth workers have to face both towards the young people they work with and provide for and towards this policy driven funding/commissioning system.

ACTIVITY 7.2

- *What do you think about this idea of having to demonstrate your results in order to win resources?*

- *What arrangements are in place in your organisation for doing this?*

- *What benefits do you think this process brings both to providers and to users of services for young people?*

Setting clear expectations and negotiating terms

If your project or centre wins a commission, this is likely to be the subject of a contract or service level agreement. There are benefits to both the commissioners and those being commissioned: expectations are clear on both sides and there should be no confusion about what is to be provided and on what terms. There should be absolute clarity about the tasks that are to be done, the activities provided, the intended outcomes and what measures are to be put in place to ensure that these are properly monitored (see Chapter 6). It is imperative that you only sign up to any agreement if you are confident that you will have all the resources you will need to provide the service and produce the outcomes. It is no use complaining afterwards that the work was under-resourced. If it is, you should not sign up to it.

It is clearly implied from this that you need to have developed effective negotiating skills to engage in a contract or service level agreement. And if you cannot agree to what the commissioner wants, it is prudent to have an alternative in your negotiation strategy. You have to know when to introduce this as an option on the table – probably at a point where it is clear that the deal on the original proposal is not going to be closed.

You should also be aware of which factors are going to weigh most heavily with the commissioners. They are looking for the project that offers the standard of service they want at a price that they can afford. They should not necessarily be going for the cheapest option. They should be securing the one that offers best value: a proper balance between quality and cost (see Chapter 6 for further discussion on quality, cost and other factors).

If you and your organisation are to be taken seriously as a provider and to be a contender in the market place, then you need to be able to demonstrate a number of important things.

- You are a team worth investing in; that means you have people with the qualifications, experience, knowledge and skills to do the job required at a good enough standard to meet requirements. This means not just having CVs in place and up to date but also having available references and testimonials to the quality of work you have done.

- Your project or centre is a serious organisation with all the necessary policies and procedures in place, not just written down in manuals but actively carried out in your day-to-day business. This includes the obvious ones such as health and safety, a criminal records check and child protection procedures; and the less obvious such as a compliments and complaints record which shows, in the case of the complaint, what its substance was, who made it, when, what was done about it, any implications for the operating procedures of the organisation, and when the complainant was notified about the action taken (see 'Setting up infrastructures' in Chapter 6).

- Your project is willing to work in partnership with another or more if between you it is possible to demonstrate that you can provide a fuller service to young people that gives better value.

- Some evidence of the impact of the work you do on the young people, their families and communities. You have to be able to show that you can make a difference. The commissioners should be convinced by a combination of qualitative (case studies and 'stories') and quantitative (data) evidence (see 'Monitoring, evaluation and reporting' in Chapter 6). It is helpful if you and your team can readily put these in front of them.

Commissioning the youth offer

The Government introduced Section 507B of the Education Act 1996 which was inserted by Section 6 of the Education and Inspections Act 2006. This received Royal Assent on 8 November 2006 and Section 6 was commenced on 8 January 2007. In England, under this legislation (introduced in 2007) all local authorities and their partners are required to make a youth offer as an entitlement to all 13 to 19 year olds in their area. This consists of four elements:

- positive activities for all young people;

- targeted youth support for those at risk or who have additional needs;

- information, advice and guidance for all young people;

- the active involvement of young people in shaping, providing and reviewing services and opportunities.

Procurement

This is a technical term referring to a part of the commissioning cycle – see page 100 – when invitations to tender are circulated, bids assessed and services are purchased from suppliers or providers.

It is possible that all the services contained within this offer will not be commissioned – some may be retained 'in-house' by existing providers. It is certainly expected that positive activities will be commissioned.

It may be that local authorities will determine that the targeted youth support is not put out to tender but is managed through locality-based integrated service teams by the local authority and its partners, including, for example, the schools and the primary care trust.

When it comes to targeted youth support, the boot may be on the other foot for commissioning services. You may find yourself commissioning youth work interventions. You may be identified as a lead professional overseeing a programme of support and development for particular young people who have been identified as at risk and then 'targeted'. This means you are trained in the use of the Common Assessment Framework. The lead professional's task is to identify a programme of prevention and intervention which will enable the young person identified as in need of this support to move from being at risk to being out of risk, or from being excluded to becoming included in service provision. This programme is likely to consist of different activities and interventions which have to be coordinated. This may entail a particular service provider, such as an outdoor adventure specialist, being commissioned to run a series of activities in which this young person takes part, along with others in the area for whom the same programme is deemed appropriate. So here you as youth worker are acting as a commissioner of particular services or activities for a young person or a designated group of young people who stand to benefit.

Commissioning poses managers of youth work with both threats and opportunities. If you are on the receiving end of commissioning, there may be a number of threats. These might include having your work given away to others who may be seen to provide better value. There may no longer be a year-on-year guarantee that you and your colleagues will be funded for work that you have always done. You will no longer be able to protect 'your' resources because they no longer belong to you. You simply have the resources for the duration of the contract or agreement. This makes investment in the project or organisation's infrastructure problematic unless you include that in some way in your costs. The risk is that if you do so, there might be a danger of pricing yourself out of the process altogether.

If you are on the giving end – that is, commissioning work – there are also dangers. For example, you may have responsibility for the outcomes of an intervention but no control over it. You rely on others and you may not have any direct line-management responsibility for them. Therefore if things are slipping, you may not be in a strong enough position to rectify matters. Delegation brings benefits but also risks.

As commissioner it is important that you have open channels of communication so that the flow of information is rapid and clear. You have to know what is going on at the time you need to know it. Arms-length management or delegation also entails building relationships of trust and reciprocity between the commissioner and the commissioned. These are built over time and through the experience of working together, sometimes finding common purpose in adversity. (This is not to suggest that you invite adversity, only to comment that it can have unifying properties.) It is also important that those being commissioned report frequently and accurately on how they are progressing; and that the commissioner as far as possible visits the project or centre to see the work happening in situ. It is important at all times to have valid evidence that demonstrates the benefits of the work to the user of the service and the value of the work to those who invest in it. So the mantra should be "evidence, evidence, evidence!" (see 'Monitoring, evaluation and reporting' in Chapter 6).

Other aspects of commissioning

It is important to recognise that the full commissioning process is more than procurement. If the commissioners, who may also be known as the Children's Trust, are doing their job properly, they will have an eye to completing the full cycle of commissioning, which entails completing the following stages in a logical sequence:

- Having a vision of what is to be secured, a long-term strategy and an *action plan*. This is usually derived from local area agreements and existing service strategies, which will be influenced by national and local priorities.

- *Needs analysis*, which again should already have been undertaken by local service providers in close consultation with service users – young people, their families and communities. This will also incorporate data drawn from local demographic studies.

- Having some kind of *supply map* of existing services. Most organisations will already have a directory of some kind showing what services and activities they offer.

- *Gap analysis* in which the differences between what services are providing and what appears to be needed can be set out.

- *Prioritising developments* when commissioners have a limited level of resources to provide all the services and activities as well as fill any gaps that are identified. Decisions will have to be taken concerning which are the most important.

- *Procurement*, meaning:
  - publicising the projects, services and activities the commissioners want to see;
  - inviting providers to tender;
  - selecting the providers;
  - issuing the contracts based on the cases being made and the extent to which applicants best meet the requirements of the tender specification;
  - agreeing the contract or service level agreement;
  - allocating the resources accordingly.

- *Monitoring progress* against intended outcomes, which will include reports from service providers on key indicators and periodic visits from commissioners or their agents to verify the evidence.

- *Reviewing* contracts and *evaluating* the whole process against the annual plan before producing an annual plan for the following year.

See the commissioning framework for *Every Child Matters* (2006).

Figure 7.1 The commissioning cycle

> ### ACTIVITY 7.3
>
> - *What benefits do you think that commissioning will bring to young people?*
>
> - *What problems and opportunities can you see with the commissioning process?*
>
> - *How might youth workers and young people become positively involved in the commissioning process?*

Managing performance

Targets are a way of managing performance and have been introduced into public services over the last 20 years, drawing on a practice that has long been established in the private sector. Specific targets are set for achieving particular policy goals, such as the levels of attainment in numeracy and literacy in schools or the numbers on waiting lists for surgical operations in hospitals. By raising the first and lowering the second, the services achieve government policy priorities.

This all sounds like common sense but the problem is that sometimes targets can be set which may be in conflict with each other. For example, it may be possible to reduce waiting-list numbers by shortening the length of time that patients stay in hospital. However, this may result in readmissions which raise costs. So by achieving one target it is possible to miss another.

Targets can lead to the creation of what are called 'perverse incentives' (de Bruijn, 2001). This is where an unintended and undesirable effect runs counter to the policy objectives. For example, if a police service is judged and funded according to its arrest rate, then resources will be put into 'feeling collars' rather than crime prevention – a priority of policing. If a school is judged by the number of pupils who achieve Level 2 (five GCSE passes at grades A*–C), then a lot of resources may be invested in work with those pupils who are on the borderline between grades C and D in order to improve the overall score at this benchmark. This means that proportionally less resources may be directed towards those below this grade who arguably need more or towards the gifted and talented who may not be stretched enough to achieve their potential.

In youth work, local authorities and their partners were given targets to reach in Resourcing Excellent Youth Services (DfES, 2002). These were soon to be misleadingly called best value performance indicators, such as the percentage of young people aged 13–19 in an area with whom youth workers were in contact (Flint, 2005). A second target was to ensure that those who were using youth work services achieved certain kinds of outcome such as accredited awards. Some youth workers reported that the second target ran counter to the first because the numbers using the service might well be diminished if young people felt under pressure to achieve, making the experience 'more like school'. In the most recent announcement on national targets for youth work (Public Service Agreement 14, 2007), accredited and recorded outcomes do not feature but have been replaced by an increase in participation in positive activities (more on this in Chapter 8). However, numbers of local authorities appear to be choosing to retain a focus on such targets (Davies and Merton, 2009).

ACTIVITY 7.4

- *Do you think it is a good idea to have targets?*

- *If so, what sort of targets do you think will help the service to reach substantial numbers of young people, including those who are notoriously hard to reach?*

- *Do you think it is a good idea to have a target to engage young people who are said to be hard to reach?*

- *What are the possible outcomes?*

- *What do you think is behind this?*

Performance management also means making judgements about what are sometimes referred to as the three Es (Ford et al., 2005): the economy, efficiency and effectiveness of a service or project.

Economy refers to the cost of the inputs used – the staff, the buildings, the equipment and materials to name the most important. When resources are finite – which they always are – minimising costs often becomes a service priority. This prompts questions such as:

- How much do different inputs cost?

- Are these inputs necessary to achieving our purposes?

- If so, can they be obtained at less cost?

- Are these resources properly controlled?

Efficiency is about the relationship between inputs and outputs. For example, how much is being produced as a result of the interaction of the inputs and young people through youth work interventions. An example of an output is the numbers of young people who have taken part in a youth exchange. This prompts questions such as:

- Are we making the best use of the resources we have?

- Has the maximum output been achieved from a particular input?

- Can the throughput from the service or intervention be improved without sacrificing quality or adding to costs?

Effectiveness is about producing results, the kinds of longer-term outcomes that policy makers are seeking: young people who are healthy, stay safe, enjoy and achieve, make a positive contribution to their communities and achieve economic wellbeing. There are two broad categories of outcome: a change of state or situation and a change of behaviour. The first kind could be a number of young people who are not in education, employment or training becoming engaged in learning or work. The second kind could be young people who are at risk of offending changing their activities or friendship patterns so they no longer hang around with the wrong crowd and choose to get themselves fit rather than get themselves arrested. Both these changes can be induced by good youth work.

Effectiveness concerns the relationship between intended and actual outcomes and prompts questions such as:

- Has the service or intervention achieved what was expected and hoped for?

- What benefits have been gained and for whom?

- What feedback and other forms of evidence have been acquired in order to inform judgements?

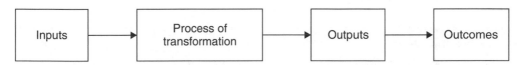

Figure 7.2 A performance model

See the commissioning framework for *Every Child Matters* (2006).

Figure 7.2 depicts an open systems model to understand and monitor performance of a service. This involves identifying inputs, the process of transforming inputs into outputs, and the outcomes these can lead to (see reference to open systems theory in Chapter 3).

Inputs are what goes into providing the service, usually the people, plant and pounds, including the knowledge and skills of staff and the resources invested in them. The cost of the inputs gives a measure of the *economy* of the activity.

The *process of transformation* is the variety of methods used in our interventions with young people – the heart of most youth work.

The *outputs* are the measure of the activity that has taken place, such as the range of the activities (e.g. those on a residential programme) and the levels of achievement of the young people who take part. The volume of the outputs divided by the cost of the inputs gives a measure of the *efficiency* of the activity.

The *outcomes* are the results or impact of the services on the lives of the young people who use them. This might include progression to training or employment, or better health or more stable relationships. They also include the results of services for the wider community, such as raising standards of attainment in schools or declining incidents of youth offending. The number and quality of the outcomes give a measure of the *effectiveness* of the organisation or service.

ACTIVITY 7.5

- *Can you think of a situation where you have intervened to produce an output and this resulted in one of the two kinds of outcome just referred to?*

- *What kinds of outputs have you or your organisation achieved with young people?*

- *What kinds of outcome could these outputs be linked to?*

As well as the three Es mentioned above, it can be important to use a fourth E in measuring and managing performance – *Equity*. In this case, we mean providers should be judged on the degree of equality of access to services. *Environment* is a fifth E meaning sustainability. For more information about the above terms see 'Monitoring, evaluating and recording' of projects in Chapter 6. See also Chapter 3 on single loop learning to contextualise the use of the three Es.

ACTIVITY 7.6

- *Do all young people in your area, regardless of, for instance, gender, race, sexuality or ability, have the same degree of access to youth clubs, centres and projects?*

- *Or are there barriers for some that prevent them taking part on equal terms?*

It is important to distinguish between targets and results and in any negotiation for a contract you should try to be clear about which you are going to be judged by. A *target* is something you aim at – it gives a general direction in which your service or project should be heading. A *result* is what your service or target achieves, whether intended or unintended. A contract might contain a target but that does not necessarily mean that you will be rewarded or not according to whether you reach it.

A contract might specify the results the client expects you to achieve, some of which may be anticipated and others not. It is important that the target does not become so important that the work of the service or project becomes distorted from its key purpose for which it has been established and resourced. For example, schools exist to provide young people with education, and with opportunities to acquire the knowledge and skills needed for a productive and contented life. They are not *responsible for* children's weight and levels of fitness, for their safety in the community and for their family's solvency, although they may *contribute to* them.

There is always a risk that in seeking resources to continue and sustain your work you may be tempted to adapt your practice and working methods to achieve different kinds of results to those that your project or service was set up for. If this becomes a pattern, your work can become subject to what is referred to as 'mission drift'. Its distinctive contribution for which it is regarded may become diluted or diverted. However, if it becomes clear that sponsors of the work no longer value the distinctive contribution you have always made, then a conscious change of mission or direction could become a prudent manoeuvre for you to consider!

Working with others

Stakeholders

Policy makers have made it clear that local authorities can only provide and commission an integrated youth offer with partners, in particular with organisations and services in the voluntary and community sector. All partners are stakeholders in youth work but not all stakeholders are partners. What is the difference?

A *stakeholder* is any individual, group or organisation that has a material, legal or political interest in your organisation and may be affected by its activities and performance. This will include young people and parents, for example, and organisations which may not have a direct responsibility for young people but who have a concern for them and their communities. An example might be faith organisations or employers. Elected members or councillors are also stakeholders because they decide priorities in public services and how resources shall be used in pursuit of them. Regional government offices are stakeholders too; they represent government interests in the regions and monitor how partners are implementing policies that may have been determined in Whitehall. They want to be kept informed of ways in which local authorities and their partners are taking these forward and how successfully the outcomes being sought are actually being achieved. Perhaps the most important stakeholder group of all is the young people themselves.

A *partner* is any service provider or agency whose activities and responsibilities affect young people directly; this could be schools and colleges, the police, the health service, a leisure or sports centre. A partner is also any other organisation that may be working with you on a project, perhaps sharing the funding that is available. Voluntary and community organisations may be stakeholders or partners or both; examples would include uniformed and non-uniformed youth organisations, sports clubs and centres, youth theatres, village youth clubs.

As a youth worker you will want to know what stakeholders think about what young people need and how you can provide for them in partnership with other services and agencies. This means undertaking some kind of analysis of your stakeholders, learning about their roles and responsibilities, finding out what they want from you and telling them what you want from them so you can reach some accommodation of each other's interests and concerns. You may decide that there is some mutual benefit in working closely with a stakeholder on a particular activity, in which both partners can add value to each other's work by bringing to it an extra dimension or resource. In this instance the stakeholder becomes a partner.

A stakeholder analysis entails close consultation with the stakeholders. You may have some ideas about what a particular stakeholder wants from your project or organisation and it will be important to check these out. In doing so, other opportunities for co-operation may be raised.

Stakeholders may not be concerned about the work you do so much on a day-to-day basis. But it is wise to keep them informed of any major developments in your project or organisation and of the results you achieve. In particular it makes sense to keep them up to date about new initiatives and achievements. This does not necessarily involve a lot of extra work. Ensuring they are included in emails or they are informed through notices on the organisation's website should not entail a great deal of expense or time. It is an important way of maintaining your profile and staying on their radar. This is essential if you want stakeholders to invest politically or financially in your work and bring greater benefits to the young people you serve.

But why co-operate anyway? Simply because it may be a requirement of a funding bid or tender that you are working in partnership with another organisation in pursuit of project objectives. It also makes sense to do so because we know that many young people have a whole range of issues and challenges they have to deal with as they grow up and many of these are interconnected.

CASE STUDY

Falling between the cracks?

Darren, a 15-year-old boy, is hacked off with school and feels he is not gaining anything from attending except grief from his teachers and peers. He comes from a home which has gained little from education and does not believe it is of much value. The mother wants the boy to help at home and is happy to collude with Darren bunking off. He hangs around with older lads who get into trouble with local shopkeepers and residents for anti-social behaviour. He has learned how to break into cars and use them for joy-riding. Darren may be getting into drink and soft drugs and engaging in petty theft to finance his habit. It is clear that the boy is at risk and that no single agency can help him tackle these risks on its own.

ACTIVITY 7.7

- *In this scenario which services and agencies could be brought together to work out a plan of prevention or intervention which will minimise the risks to Darren?*

- *Under whose authority might this be done?*

- *What would partner services and organisations be seeking to do?*

- *To whom should they be accountable?*

Partnerships

There are both advantages and some disadvantages in working closely with partners in providing support and development opportunities or positive activities for young people. One advantage would be to provide a wider range of opportunities and a network of support for the young person or group of young people. A disadvantage is that the more organisations and people that become involved, the longer it takes to agree decisions about resources, methods, sharing information and claiming credit, and taking responsibility for the results.

If you are involved in running a youth project or centre that involves partnership work, you have to take account of certain factors in making sure the partnership works. There are five tests of a good partnership and it is worth asking to what extent you are satisfying them.

1 Does the partnership lead to *improvement in the quality and range of services*?

2 Does the partnership provide *good value for money*?

3 Does the partnership create *new thinking* that challenges and changes service provision?

4 Does the partnership bring *benefits to more vulnerable groups* and communities so they achieve better outcomes?

5 Does the partnership *alter the balance of power* between service providers and service users in favour of the latter?

If you can muster evidence to show that these conditions are being met, then the partnership is definitely worth maintaining. If you cannot, then you might want to establish further reasons for maintaining the partnership. If your project is meeting some tests but not others, you might devise a plan for improving the partnership and the benefits it brings.

Managing work that involves partnerships is difficult, demanding but worthwhile. It requires open and clear channels of communication between partners so that information, ideas and insights can be shared and used to everybody's benefit. Poor communication breeds mistrust. It is important to keep people 'in the loop'. Sometimes you may have responsibility but no power in running a partnership project. In this case you need to exercise and develop your influencing skills (see Chapter 8).

Partnerships can be time-intensive. Like any relationship which involves a degree of interdependence, a partnership needs nourishing and strengthening. Nothing should be taken for granted and assumptions should be checked out. You must be aware of the dangers of presuming that partners know, understand and agree something. It is worth making sure they do before you take a decision because if they find out something has happened that they were not aware of, they can feel manipulated and then a level of mistrust can set in. Once that has happened, a call on your diplomatic skills may well be required.

Your own control and autonomy sometimes have to be sacrificed or at least compromised in some way when working in partnerships. Accountability gets spread more widely as you realise that you may have to report for your actions not just to your own management committee but also less directly to others as well. In addition you have to be aware that sometimes decisions and actions you take in your project or organisation that do not have a *direct* bearing on the work you are doing in partnership with others may have some *indirect* impact. Partnerships usually require you to think 'out of the box' and beyond your usual horizons; they require a degree of empathy with the way partners think and work as well as an understanding of the pressures and imperatives that influence them.

ACTIVITY *7.8*

- *Make a list of the advantages and disadvantages you can identify with regard to working in partnership.*

- *How might you build up the advantages and tackle the disadvantages?*

Networking

Successful partnership entails effective networking. It means ensuring that you and your organisation are connected with others who are interested and active in the same field. It requires open and continuous communication through telephone, internet and attendance at meetings so that you are in the know about what is going on and how policy and practice are evolving. It means finding out where resources are, what new initiatives and funding streams are coming into play and then seeking possible partners from within the network with whom you can collaborate on a particular initiative.

Networking involves very different ways of working to the traditional methods of command and control adopted in public services. It is a much more open process relying on the free flow of information, ideas and influence where the constraints of bureaucratic procedures and regulation are weakened if not removed. It gives workers more discretion and room for manoeuvre in their day-to-day work but should not obstruct accountability. It means that the accountability is more diffuse so that you not only report on your actions upwards to your line manager but also to others with whom you work, including partners, stakeholders and, of course, young people themselves.

CASE STUDY

Making sex safe and healthy

Roadley, a local youth centre, works closely with the nurses and medical staff in the local hospital to provide a sexual health service for young people using the centre who tend not to make use of the services provided in their local doctor's surgery or clinic. Screening for sexually transmitted infections, free condom distribution and pregnancy testing are conducted by arrangement in the youth centre. This initiative was not established as a result of any formal partnership or service level agreement; nor has it been commissioned, coordinated or controlled by senior managers. Instead the youth workers and front-line health service staff have used their common sense and networking skills to create an excellent service that is valued by the young people and that contributes to the targets that both services have been set through the local area agreement.

Effective networking means keeping your eyes and ears open to developments and innovation. It means periodically scanning the websites of organisations to keep abreast of initiatives and see what can be learned from them that could apply to your own work. It is about making connections, not just between people but also between ideas, joining up the dots to see how different policy drivers interconnect and how more holistic and joined-up approaches can be taken towards the support and development of young people.

ACTIVITY 7.9

- *Are you part of a network?*

- *Are you aware of or involved in informal arrangements somewhat like the Roadley one above?*

- *With which organisations, agencies and people are you in most frequent and direct contact?*

- *What benefits do you derive from this networking?*

- *Is it worth the investment of time and effort required?*

- *Are there others with whom you might need to engage to bring more benefits to your organisation and the young people you work with?*

Keeping matters fresh

Earlier we identified innovation as being one of the five tests of partnership when we asked whether the partnership creates *new thinking* that challenges and changes service provision. Innovation is not important for innovation's sake. But it is important if youth work wants to be at the leading edge of services for young people. One of the unique selling points of youth workers is their ability to get alongside young people, build relationships of trust and mutual regard with them, understand their condition and situation and pick up on what they need and want if they are going to make the most of opportunities and make progress in their lives.

Innovation in relation to youth work means activity that:

- breaks new ground and pushes back the boundaries of professional knowledge and practice;

- develops the capacity of young people and youth workers for original ideas and action;

- fosters creative achievement that adds value to the quality and range of work.

Innovation involves professional risk-taking, combining the freedom to experiment with the use of proven skills, knowledge and understanding. It may draw on the ideas and achievement of others so as to adapt and apply them in new ways.

Innovation is the hallmark of a responsive service. To use a business analogy, innovation requires responses to emerging needs and coming up with a new product or service. It is sometimes taken to mean using an existing one in a new location – for example, youth provision in Youth Offending Institutions. A new setting can alter or perhaps transform the product. It can also mean youth workers operating in new arenas or supporting other professionals in theirs – for example, as members of Youth Offending Teams trying to reduce the risk of youth crime or as personal advisers providing support to young people as part of the Connexions service.

Innovation could and should be sustainable. It often attracts special funding because government or some other sponsor wants to back youth work that can be shown to 'make a difference' and provide solutions to problems that other services cannot. If you try something new and it is successful, then it should be replicated and absorbed within the main bloodstream of the service. At this point, its claim to be innovative might be forfeited. Yet that does not mean the work ceases to be dynamic or effective. A learning organisation will absorb the lessons of innovation, disseminate them and apply them within its networks (for more about learning organisations see Chapter 3).

There is also a view that innovation is no different from effective youth work, but equating innovation with effectiveness is probably mistaken. Certainly innovative work can be effective but is not in all cases. Moreover, there are many examples of effective youth work which are by no means innovative. For example, providing alternative programmes based on youth work principles for disaffected school pupils has been taking place for 30 years;

Table 7.1 Factors contributing towards and obstructing innovation

Factors contributing towards innovation (Merton, 2001)	Factors obstructing innovation
Accepting uncertainty	Emphasis on short-term results and gains
Strongly committed individuals prepared to challenge the status quo, take risks and have a go at something different	Highly controlling management; excessive rules and regulations
Accepting controversy and contest	Conforming behaviour expecting people to do as they are told
Lateral thinking; working 'outside the box' and across professional boundaries	Excessive rationalism; expecting things to happen in a logical, pre-determined pattern
Knowledge, responsiveness, openness, shared values, creative staff recognising each others' skills	Cautious, competitive and mistrustful staff unwilling to share knowledge and skills
Willing to trust partners in other agencies and contribute to broader policy agenda	Reluctance to engage in multi-agency initiatives or make resources available for broader policy purposes
Acceptance of initial costs	Over-emphasis on early accurate costs
Need and determination to (a) find a new focus and interest in the work; (b) find radical responses to issues	Contentment with status quo
Preparedness to work from young people's perspectives and concerns	Adults setting the agenda

what is different now is the high-policy profile given to inclusion and the consequent legitimisation of such youth work interventions. Innovation must mean 'new' or it means nothing.

You may feel sceptical about innovation perhaps because it commands a great deal of attention and, consequently, resources. This is understandable if it does so at the expense of effective mainstream provision but if innovation can demonstrate new ways of making a difference to the lives of young people and their communities, then it can be justifiably recognised, rewarded and replicated. If mainstream provision is producing good results, retaining it may require you to re-cast descriptions and presentations of it in terms that 'hit the right buttons' and with references to buzz-phrases that are prevalent in policy making at the time.

Innovation is the means of change. Youth organisations which need to change what they do sometimes find it difficult because much is invested in their existing culture. There is often resistance to taking the risks which inevitably are part of change. Elected members as much as officers find it hard to sanction and support new ways of undertaking the work, even when they can see that existing methods are not proving effective. It might be helpful to identify some of the factors that seem to be key in determining whether or not innovation is likely to occur.

Innovation can also bring you competitive advantage over other agencies and services. If there is a long-standing problem or issue facing young people in your area, you may be more likely to win the resources for dealing with it if you can demonstrate that your approach is new and that you will use methods which have not been applied locally before.

Demonstrating results and public value

How do you know whether your work is making a difference and how can you show people when it is? These are crucial questions in managing yourself and your work in the contemporary policy context. Why? Because those who provide the funds and make the policies want and have the right to know. And if you cannot tell them, then you forfeit your entitlement to your share of the limited resources that are available.

One reason why government has introduced targets in public services is to give providers a clear idea of what is expected of them. As indicated earlier, targets have their uses but only if they are proportionate and do not obstruct you from achieving your core purposes. We have already explained that sometimes targets can create perverse incentives or distort an organisation's core purpose, in which case you can hit the target but miss the point. Increasingly, service providers are being asked through the commissioning process to set targets themselves. This requires careful judgement because if you set the targets too high, then you are unlikely to achieve them, and if you set them too low, you may risk not getting the work.

It is important to show that the work you are doing has public value and that it brings benefits to users of services and adds to the wellbeing of the wider community. Youth work has often provided the glue in communities, what academics, researchers and policy makers refer to sometimes as *social capital* by building stronger, more sustainable communities where people feel safe, have a sense of belonging, do things for themselves and for each other, and participate as active citizens. Youth workers thereby also make an important contribution to *social inclusion*.

There are said to be two forms of social capital (drawn from the work of Robert Putnam, notably *Bowling Alone*, 2000):

- *bonding* social capital, which brings people of similar attitudes and dispositions together, sometimes to the exclusion of others;

- *bridging* social capital, which seeks to bring together people of outwardly different attitudes and dispositions, out of recognition that there will be mutual benefit and what they share may be more important than what differentiates them.

Bridging social capital is important in the context of young people's development, in particular those who come from disadvantaged communities. Young people's potential can be limited by the narrowness of their immediate environment. Youth workers can help to make these boundaries more elastic and can open up young people to contacts, networks and opportunities where their skills and qualities can be expressed and developed. In combination with other opportunities, youth work offers alternative routes to greater independence to those conventionally provided by education and the labour market.

Of course these kinds of outcomes are hard to measure. Is it possible to weigh or count positive relationships, trust, compassion or solidarity? Of course not, which is why policy makers and funders resort to the metrics of targets, such as the number of young people achieving accredited or recorded outcomes. These are inevitably narrower rather than broader community benefits such as social capital and, if they become the primary objective of your interventions, they can have a restricting impact on the ways in which youth workers relate to young people.

Whatever your views of the merits and drawbacks of targets and performance measures, it is necessary that you understand why they are important and that you are familiar with some of the ways in which they can be used to demonstrate impact. We can refer you to a number of different ways in which this is done in the public sector generally and in services for young people more particularly. One of the key thinkers whose approach is having considerable impact on providers of services for children and young people is Mark Friedman, an American who has devised a very simple method to use frameworks for providing outcome-based accountability. He asks three straightforward and important questions:

- How much was done?

- How well was it done?

- Is anyone better off?

In relation to the third he distinguishes between qualitative data and quantitative data. This is best represented in Friedman's quadrant (see Chapter 6).

ACTIVITY 7.10

- *Under the headings of Friedman's grid on page 88 in Chapter 6, what questions does it make most sense for you and your organisation to ask?*

- *How easily can you collect the answers?*

- *What management information do you hold that will easily produce what you need to give a satisfactory answer?*

There are three other questions that as a youth worker you need to have answers to if you are to demonstrate that the work you do has public value:

- Who benefits from the work?

- In what ways do they benefit?

- In which circumstances do they benefit most and why?

You will need to have reliable evidence to support any judgements or statements you make in reply to these questions.

If you can manage to collect evidence that is sufficient, reliable, up to date and accurate, then you have to think about how to get that across to the people you want to influence, including those who make decisions about where scarce resources are to be allocated. For this you will need to have a *communication plan*. This is quite straightforward. It needs to convey simple messages to key audiences at times which you consider to be most fitting. For example, if you have a good story to tell about your service or organisation which shows the positive outcomes achieved by young people and the benefits these bring to the local community, then the best time to produce these findings may be in the immediate weeks leading up to the budget-setting round of meetings in the local authority.

The communication plan should have a simple format which sets out the key messages you want to convey with the supporting data to back them up, the key audiences you want to influence, the timing of the messages and the person(s) responsible for delivering them. It is helpful if those people who have been directly involved in the work itself have direct involvement in and responsibility for shaping the messages, including young people. Positive messages can do much to raise morale and enhance performance. They can in this way increase the prospect of securing additional resources and then producing even better results and more positive messages next time.

CHAPTER REVIEW

In this chapter we have shown how policy changes have led to a much more business-like culture in which public services, including youth work, now operate. This has meant that much closer attention is paid to how services perform with respect to:

- better outcomes for young people;

- new processes, such as commissioning, which are intended to introduce more competition and therefore efficiencies into 'the market' of positive activities;

- new relationships such as collaboration and networking which might soften some of the harder competitive edges of the market place and enable individual services to achieve more for young people with others than they can on their own;

- the requirement on services to demonstrate their impact and public value.

These developments have in turn placed new demands and expectations on people working at all levels in services for young people. They are proving something of a challenge, and those services that are capable of meeting it might reasonably expect to be rewarded with higher levels of resourcing. Or as government puts it 'invest and reform', although it might be more realistic to acknowledge that services will have to reform before they can expect to receive the levels of investment to which they aspire.

FURTHER READING

Friedman, M (2005) *Trying hard is not good enough: How to produce measurable improvements for customers and communities.* Victoria, Canada: Trafford Publishing.

For current information about commissioning refer to the government website Better Outcomes: Commissioning for Children and Young People, intended to create a community of practice for Children's Trusts that will facilitate shared learning, sharing of good practice and joint problem-solving: **www.commissioningsupport.org.uk/about_commissioning.aspx**

Department for Children, Schools and Families (2008) Statutory guidance on section 507B Education Act 1996. Online: **www.dcsf.gov.uk/localauthorities/index.cfm?action= content&contentID=13319&categoryID=75&subcategoryID=106**

USEFUL WEBSITES

Office of the Third Sector **www.cabinetoffice.gov.uk/third_sector.aspx**

Department of Communities and Local Government **www.communities.gov.uk/communities/thirdsector/**

REFERENCES

Joint Planning and Commissioning Framework for Children, Young People and Maternity Services (2006) *Every child matters.* London: DfES. Online: **www.everychildmatters.gov.uk**

Davies, B and Merton, B (2009) *Squaring the circle? Findings of a 'modest inquiry' into the state of youth work practice in a changing policy environment.* Online: **www.dmu.ac.uk/Images/Squaring% 20the%20Circle_tcm6-50166.pdf**

De Bruijn, H (2002) *Managing performance in the public sector.* London: Routledge.

Department for Children, Schools and Families (2008) *Statutory guidance on section 507B Education Act 1996 on positive activities.* London: DCSF.

Department for Education and Skills (2002) *Resourcing excellent youth services.* London: DfES.

Flint, W (2005) *Recording young people's progress and accreditation in youth work.* Leicester: NYA (available from **www.nya.org.uk**).

Flynn, N (2007) *Public sector management,* 5th edition. London: Prentice Hall.

Ford, K, Hunter, R, Merton, B and Waller, D (2005) *Leading and managing youth work and services for young people.* Leicester: The National Youth Agency.

Friedman, M (2005) *Trying hard is not good enough: How to produce measurable improvements for customers and communities.* Victoria, Canada: Trafford Publishing.

Merton, B (2001) *So, what's new: innovation in youth work.* Leicester: The National Youth Agency.

Putnam, R (2000) *Bowling alone – the collapse and revival of American community.* New York: Simon and Schuster.

Public Service Agreement 14 (2007)

Chapter 8

Managing in a complex and fast-changing policy environment

Bryan Merton

Achieving your Youth and Community Work degree

This chapter is about policy and its implications for youth work services. It will help you to meet the following National Occupational Standards (February 2008).

- *4.1.1 Investigate the needs of young people and the community in relation to youth work*

- *4.1.2 Evaluate and prioritise requirements for youth work activities from your organisation*

- *4.2.2 Develop a strategic plan for youth work*

Introduction

We begin this chapter by explaining why it is important for youth workers to understand the big picture and develop a perspective on policy if they are to influence the nature, range and quality of services provided for young people on the ground, and to maximise their central position responding simultaneously to policy and to young people and others in the communities with whom they work. We stress the value and importance of actively involving young people and their communities in the process and the rationale behind ensuring that services are locally determined. We reassert the importance policy makers attach to joining things up and some of the implications this emphasis has for leading and managing services. We conclude with a focus on dealing with complexity at every level and developing skills of influence and persuasion.

Getting the big picture

Why should youth workers be concerned about policy? Surely the job of the youth worker is to make relationships with young people and support them in their development in whatever ways seem most appropriate. But how you work with young people is determined by a number of factors, one of the most significant being the current policy framework which shapes the publicly funded services provided.

Youth work is not a policy-free zone. Nor should it be because policy matters. It matters because it says a great deal about how society views and values young people and their best interests. And those who work directly with young people are in a strong position to influence the policy that shapes their work. Why? Because they know well the experiences, hopes, aspirations, fears and worries that affect young people as they develop. They know what concerns them and what interests them. And it is important that any policies and priorities that are created for young people take account of them. The best advocates for young people are young people themselves. The second best are those workers with whom they can build relationships of trust.

So youth policy and its continuous evolution is important. It also matters that those who work with young people have policy memory – that they know where policy comes from and why. It does not just come out of the ether. Policy is made by men and women and it is shaped by the circumstances and conditions of the time. It is important that front-line workers understand this and that is why the youth work profession is fortunate to have its evolution and development over the last 60 years chronicled by Bernard Davies (1999a, 1999b, 2008).

ACTIVITY *8.1*

- *As a youth worker do you get involved in making policy at local level?*

- *How do you ensure it takes account of the needs and aspirations of the young people you work with?*

- *What examples can you give of ways in which you have been able to influence policy?*

Influencing policy locally

The policy framework that governs the nature, range and quality of services for young people, including youth work, is set by national government but the local authorities and their partners that actually provide these services contribute significantly too. Priorities are currently established through Local Area Agreements, and how much resource is allocated to these services and, more specifically, how these resources are deployed is also determined locally. The interplay between national policy as expressed through consultation (DfES, 2005/2006) and subsequent legislation, and strategic planning decisions made by local government officers and elected members leads to the provision made through clubs, centres and projects in neighbourhoods and across services – the kind of provision you are involved in.

In the last few years there has been a considerable degree of government interest in youth policy. For example, in 2007 Her Majesty's Treasury and the new Department of Children, Schools and Families (DCSF) combined to produce a new and unprecedented ten-year youth strategy (DCSF, 2007). As a further illustration of attempts to join up thinking across Whitehall, the Youth Justice Board, previously housed in the Home Office, was transferred to the new Department for Children, Schools and Families. And later in 2007 the government introduced PSA (Public Service Agreement) 14 that has as its objective to increase the number of children and young people on the path to success. This PSA established a set of indicators agreed between central and local government that will be overseen and monitored by the nine Regional Government Offices in England. There are five indicators.

1 Reduce the proportion of 16 to 18 year olds who are not in education, employment or training.

2 More participation in positive activities.

3 Reduce the proportion of young people using illicit drugs, alcohol or volatile substances.

4 Reduce the under-18 conception rate.

5 Reduce the number of first-time entrants into the criminal justice system aged 10–17.

It is important to recognise that while the terms, conditions and systems for shaping policy making between Whitehall and Town Hall may change, the underlying principle of jointly taking responsibility for determining the provision of services will not.

All this may seem to be removed by some distance from the day-to-day concerns of youth workers and their managers responsible for ensuring that there are activities and services for young people to take part in locally. They are required to make provision based on a thorough and detailed assessment of needs in localities and this assessment should be undertaken by the local authority and its partners, including young people themselves. The provision established as a result of this assessment should be set out in the local children and young people's plan.

The most recent policy statement (DCSF, 2008) that has been issued emphasises the importance of ensuring that provision is made by a wide range of suppliers, including those in the voluntary and community sector and the private sector as well as by the local authority. Government has also urged that every effort must be made to reduce barriers to access to provision. These barriers have in the past tended to mean that those who stand to gain most from the opportunities do not avail themselves of them.

This should help to challenge the tendency for well-established patterns of provision to remain, even though there are cases where they may not be well used by young people and bring little benefit to local communities. For fear of losing the support of local people, councillors are sometimes reluctant to lose any provision in their constituencies even if they are providing a poor-quality service. This may be for good reason in the sense that once resources are lost to a service it is sometimes very hard to get them back in any form. As we have seen in the previous chapter, the commissioning process is intended to ensure that outdated provision and inefficient services are in effect de-commissioned. For further information on what government expects of local authorities and their partners, carefully read the guidance that has been issued (DCSF, 2008).

- *How is provision determined in your area?*
- *Is the thumbprint of national policy and Local Area Agreements evident in the local youth offer?*
- *How have you been involved in assessing needs and in identifying gaps?*
- *Have young people been involved and in which ways?*
- *Have parents been consulted?*
- *What role do elected members play in the process?*
- *What potential benefits could emerge from the apparent threat to close a local facility?*
- *Do you think that the pattern of provision reflects what young people need and want?*

Actively involving young people

Government policy constantly reasserts the importance of gathering the views of local young people in shaping and influencing policy at national and local levels. As a youth worker you will welcome this as it represents what good youth work stands for – supporting young people in finding their place and expressing their voice in society. It is also consistent with the broader social policy objective of ensuring that the voice of service users is instrumental in determining priorities and the nature and quality of the services provided.

Policy makers also recognise that it is not always straightforward to secure the voice of those who might stand to gain most from services – those at risk and vulnerable who seem to be excluded from much provision. You have probably experienced this. It tends to be the bright, articulate, well-motivated young people who put themselves forward to take part in representative structures and processes such as youth forums and councils. While their voice is important and deserves to be heard, it can drown out the views of their less-confident peers who may have valuable things to say but lack the confidence to do so. This may be because discussion often takes place in settings and forms that the less articulate and confident find challenging – meetings with papers to read, opinions to record and decisions to note. Those who are ill at ease in these 'adult' contexts may find the internet and other forms of communication through new technology less threatening, as well as more conversational and informal opportunities to express their views.

- *What arrangements does your organisation make to manage the active involvement of young people in shaping provision locally?*
- *How successfully do they capture the voice of the less confident and articulate young people in your area?*
- *How do you ensure that disadvantaged young people have a say in the provision and activities on offer where they live?*

Going local

As our communities become more diverse and complex they present government at national and local level with new challenges. This is compounded by the speed and range of ways in which people communicate, as well as the spread and increase in information that is available and which can be used to influence opinions and decisions. Sometimes government seems very remote and the concerns of those in the inner circle seem to be out of touch with local people. Some policy makers recognise this and that is why slogans such as 'double devolution' (Weaver, 2006) have emerged as a possible response.

The rationale behind such an idea is that local people living in neighbourhoods know well what is in their interests and may in some cases know better than those who are elected to make decisions on their behalf. That is why there has been a growth in more local structures for decision making such as community councils and neighbourhood forums. And why there is greater interest and investment in social enterprises and community interest companies. These are seen to have a more organic and authentic approach to dealing with the challenges of modern living than the more ponderous and bureaucratic procedures adopted by local authorities.

Although there are clearly advantages in developing very local structures and processes for making decisions about policy priorities and resource allocation in communities, there may be disadvantages. One example could be that the vision of local people may be too narrow, particularly if they have only ever lived in one location. If they have developed social capital of a bonding kind (as described in Chapter 7), it may have led to a reluctance and resistance to newcomers and outsiders, such as travellers, refugees or asylum-seekers. If they have only ever encountered a limited number of solutions to problems, they may be unaware that others might exist. They may be unable to appreciate the 'big picture' that is sometimes needed to afford different perspectives on local situations.

An example that may be familiar to you as a youth worker is how easily communities can take against the young. The local press often demonises young people and lays many of the community's social problems at their door. All young people can be stigmatised by the behaviour of a limited number of 'trouble-makers'. More tolerant and compassionate attitudes towards the young may be resisted by older people who may feel threatened or frightened by them.

ACTIVITY *8.4*

- *What do you see as the advantages and disadvantages of double devolution – of pushing decision making down to the grass roots?*

- *What do you know of intergenerational misunderstanding and conflict in neighbourhoods where you work or have worked?*

- *What do you think can be done to reduce it?*

Making services available

Policy changes fast and in such a volatile environment it is hard to keep up. For example, the last six years has seen the launch of a Change for Children programme which has sought to make services more locally responsive and to join them up better so that children and young people's needs are treated holistically and no one is in danger of falling through the net.

For those young people who are deemed to be 'at risk', more targeted services have been introduced and these include teams of specialist workers around the child or the young person. This policy measure is based on the assumption that in any neighbourhood there is a significant and identifiable cohort of young people who are at risk of exclusion, neglect, mistreatment and other forms of social harm. It is believed that if they are identified early enough and programmes of prevention are introduced, then there will be less cause to intervene later when the child or young person has come to the attention of the authorities because they have moved from being 'at risk' to being 'in trouble'. We will return to this later.

First though it is important to consider whether some services are best provided locally at neighbourhood level and some centrally or across a local authority. For example, it should be possible to provide in each neighbourhood, however defined, a centre providing good-quality positive activities of a recreational and informal educational kind – a place to go with things to do and people to talk to.

But when resources are limited it may not be possible for the local authority to provide each neighbourhood with a specialist centre for young people with learning difficulties and disabilities that is not school based, for example. Not everything can necessarily be replicated at neighbourhood level.

Youth work takes many different forms and that is one reason why it is challenging to manage it effectively. There are good arguments for ensuring that in each neighbourhood there should be

- a magnet centre of positive activities;

- smaller satellite provision of similar activities run by partner services and agencies;

- a team of detached and outreach workers deployed to work with young people who may not be attracted to building-based provision;

- information, advice, guidance and counselling services in schools and in the community;

- more targeted and individualised programmes for those at risk.

Managing open access, street-based and targeted provision and the traffic of young people between them is a task facing all youth workers. It is important that you encourage young people to move between different forms of provision so that they can take advantage of the full range of opportunities and networks that are available to them.

If government is serious about devolving decision making and resource allocation to neighbourhoods, then an investment in community development is essential. This means not only spending money on the physical fabric of a neighbourhood, important though this is, but also ensuring that local people develop the skills, knowledge and awareness to develop programmes and projects that meet needs and respond to aspirations. Communities do not develop overnight. The process can be slow and painstaking. Trust has to be built, relationships strengthened and alliances formed. People have to be listened to, different viewpoints reconciled and priorities negotiated and agreed. Youth work becomes more than directly working with young people. It means winning the support of families and different community groups. It has to be established in the warp and weft of the neighbourhood. This can be done but it requires patience, sensitivity and tenacity; it entails the resilience, resolve and resourcefulness that are the very qualities that you try to inspire in the young people you work with.

ACTIVITY **8.5**

- *What is the range of positive activities, services and opportunities in your area?*

- *Do young people take advantage of the full range?*

- *Are there important elements missing?*

- *Do young people move between different forms of provision and extend their network of contacts and repertoires of skills and interests?*

- *How do you help them to manage this?*

- *How do you involve the local community in supporting activities for young people in the area?*

Joining things up

As well as more local neighbourhood-based determination of priorities and provision, policy is driving local authorities and their partners to collaborate more intensively in securing more coherent, seamless services and opportunities for young people's support and development. Although this trend in social policy can be traced back to the early years of the New Labour government, it did not surface significantly for youth workers and providers of services for young people until the publication of the *Youth Matters* Green Paper in 2005. Here Integrated Youth Support Services (IYSS) were identified with the intention of making services for young people *more integrated, efficient and effective.* The paper described the development of integrated youth support services, under the leadership of local authorities, working through Children's Trusts. This would lead to a

> *single body responsible and accountable for youth policy and the Every Child Matters outcomes in each area [which will] enable integrated planning and commissioning of the full range of services for teenagers from universal activities through to more specialist and targeted support. This will lead to an integrated youth support service, focused on and structured around young people's needs and involving a wide range of providers, including voluntary and community organisations.*

(DfES, 2005)

The Children's Workforce Development Council, which has been charged with overseeing and developing the whole workforce for children and young people's services, defines integration as follows:

Integrated working is where everyone supporting children and young people works together effectively to put the child at the centre, meet their needs and improve their lives.

By combining their professional expertise, knowledge and skills, and involving the child or young person and family throughout, practitioners can identify needs earlier, deliver a coordinated package of support that is centred on the child or young person, and help to secure better outcomes for them.

Integrated working is achieved through collaboration and coordination at all levels, across all services, in both single and multi agency settings. It requires clear and strong leadership and management. It is facilitated by the adoption of common services delivery models, tools and processes.

(CWDC, 2008, p1)

The National Youth Agency and the management training and consultancy company FPM Training have jointly produced a paper in which they assert that the breadth of the definition of integration will mean that managers will have to work with partners and stakeholders in their area to agree what provision is needed. This marks a departure from the more traditional approach of a tight, usually centralised specification that leads to the implementation of policy.

Managers will need to develop the skills to work with loose and ambiguous overarching definitions and specifications. Within these broad parameters they will also need to lead and manage tightly defined programmes of action which develop and deliver services based on the needs of young people.

(Ford, 2008, para 31)

The core principles that will underpin any attempt to join up services for young people include:

- being centred on the young person;
- providing the four components of the youth offer (see Chapter 7);
- creating a focus on early intervention and prevention and providing both universal and targeted services so as to meet young people's needs;
- involving young people in planning and delivery;
- integrating leadership and management across specialist services;
- breaking down barriers between professionals delivering services to young people;
- adopting a multi-agency approach;
- achieving efficiencies through integrated delivery and economies of scale so as to redirect resources to front-line delivery;

- bringing together planning, commissioning and providing services to deliver local solutions through Children's Trusts.

On paper this all makes sense. In practice it is a lot more difficult. It is tempting to ask whether integration is a dream or it can be made to work. Would not 'closer alignment' of services be more realistic than integration? It is important to be clear about what aspects of services are meant to be joined up.

First, what kind of *processes* can be joined up? In assessing the needs of young people who have been targeted for prevention and intervention because they are judged to be at risk, it makes sense to ensure that this is done to a common framework to be used by all service providers – teachers, youth workers, social workers, education welfare officers, personal advisers and so on. Therefore the Common Assessment Framework (CAF) has been introduced and practitioners trained in its use. This is an example of the integration of a process.

Second, *resources* are meant to be pooled. There is intended to be a portion of each service's budget that is shared in the cause of integration. For example, from 2008 Youth Offending Services are meant to pool with local youth support services 10 per cent of the budget of the Youth Justice Board funding they would expect to divert to young people's preventative activities (DCSF, 2007).

Information about young people is to be shared across services and protocols introduced for this purpose. This is a controversial matter for youth workers whose relationships with young people are built on trust (Davies and Merton, 2009, p18). It may be difficult to retain this when the young people are made aware that the youth worker is required to share information with other service providers, albeit in the best interests of the young person.

Facilities should be shared including the office accommodation where the team around the young person are housed. Co-location is meant to ensure that it is easier for young people to access services ('only one door') and for practitioners to keep each other in touch and informed about what is happening with particular young people. It is questionable whether this is feasible or even necessary to enable people to work effectively together.

Skills and *insights* should also be shared and joined up so that professionals can learn from each other and perhaps in time some of the boundaries that have traditionally separated them and allowed them to develop their own 'professional identities' can be overcome. This makes some youth workers feel very nervous. Why? Because they sense that their own particular identity and methods, based on a well-honed and much-cherished set of values, may well be undermined in the drive to create a kind of hybrid 'youth professional' referred to in *Aiming High* (DCSF, 2007) and by the Children's Workforce Development Council (CWDC).

The joining up of *staff* is a contentious issue. Each profession working with young people (teachers, youth workers, social workers, personal advisers, education welfare officers, child psychologists) brings to their work a distinctive set of values, principles, insights, knowledge and skills. These have been imparted, learned and modified over the years in the light of experience and evolving statutory duties and policy imperatives. However, each contributes in a distinctive way to the support and development of young people. It is important that these different perspectives and approaches are not lost and the government recognises this. Integration does not necessarily mean a single homogenous workforce.

The key question that has to be asked in relation to this question of integration is 'Who benefits?' If it can be shown that young people get a better service that more satisfactorily meets their needs and expectations from joining things up, then the policy can be justified. If the evidence is that it makes no difference, then one has to ask whether it is worth the costly re-organisation and uncertainty that the introduction of a new policy inevitably entails. The ultimate test of policy, acknowledged by those who make it, is whether those intended to use the services and benefit from them – in this case young people and their communities – actually do use them in greater numbers and prosper from doing so. On this latter question the jury is still out, since the roll-out and implementation of integrated support and development of services for young people has yet to take hold as we write.

ACTIVITY *8.6*

- *What do you think of the idea of integrating services for young people?*

- *How does it affect you and the work you do with young people?*

- *How has the service you provide been enhanced by the process?*

- *What new skills and insights have you acquired?*

- *Is there evidence that young people get a better deal as a result?*

Dealing with complexity

It is logical to tackle interconnected problems, sometimes referred to as 'wicked issues', in joined-up ways. It is an entirely reasonable premise upon which to base a policy. However, systems are needed to handle the complexity of the issues that are involved. Many people find it difficult to operate effectively in the zone of complexity. This is because it is hard to contain a great deal of information within one's head, as well as an often complicated map of the different interests, agencies and organisations involved. Clarity is hard to come by in these situations and if you are not clear about something, it is hard to think your way through it. How then do you manage when you are working like this?

There is no simple answer but some people find it useful to draw diagrams so they can picture the different facets of an issue and how they interrelate. In this way you can see which aspects of a problem can be dealt with independently of others and which cannot. Drawing lines and arrows between different aspects can be helpful. Other people use spidergrams as a device for doing something similar because they clarify how things are connected. They can also represent how people think and some analysis of them might reveal different ways of seeing matters. This is important because a lot of problems are caused by differences in perception between people about the same things.

One of the problems you are likely to face in working in the zone of complexity – where you are asked to handle considerable amounts of information and weigh different points of view – is that you feel you should be in control of events. If you are not in control, you may feel you are falling short of what is expected. Not being in control therefore may well make you anxious and feeling too high a level of anxiety can impair your performance. (Being in control is also considered in Chapter 2 in relation to managing yourself.)

One way forward may be to stop thinking you have to be in control and instead acknowledge complexity as a way of working and respond to it as best you can. Some people always prefer to have a plan in their heads about how they will deal with a situation; that helps to reduce the anxiety of trying to handle and control too many variables. But a military strategist once said that no plan outlives engagement with the enemy. This may be true of your work too. You may have worked out how you intend to manage a situation but then when you get into it, you find it different to what you expected, or you react differently to what you find to the way you had anticipated. Your plan then immediately flies out of the window. The trick is not to panic but to perhaps just 'go with the flow' (mirroring good responsive youth work) and see where it takes you. Another plan may emerge.

Taking responsibility

Most of us are brought up to believe that we live in a fairly stable, predictable world and we have built our institutions to reflect that. Therefore we have until now experienced organisations as hierarchical, orderly, rules-based and bureaucratically administered (see Chapter 3 for more about organisations). They may be slow and sometimes cumbersome but they are consistent and *seek* to be rational in their behaviours. (It does not mean that they always are! After all, they are composed of people who are capable of responding irrationally, in particular when they feel they are under pressure.)

As technology advances, so information accumulates and moves at great speed across institutional boundaries. This means that decisions are made swiftly and institutions have had to adapt to take account of these changes. They have sought to become what are sometimes referred to as 'learning organisations' – flat (less hierarchical), fluid and flexible so that they can evolve and develop in response to what their users want and the fast-changing, complex and sometimes chaotic environment.

This has led to an abandonment in some organisations of traditional 'command and control' methods of management to new styles that seek to 'empower' staff who are close to the service user so they can make decisions for themselves without having to refer them up for approval by a 'line manager'. There has been a blurring of 'leadership' and 'management' as organisations have tried to adopt what is now referred to as more 'distributed' forms of leadership (e.g. McKimm and Held, 2009).

This devolves responsibility for making decisions further down the line with the hope and expectation that 'better' decisions will be taken. It can induce in front-line staff a degree of concern and anxiety, even ambivalence, as they both welcome and fear the added responsibilities which have been conferred upon them.

One consequence of this development is a tendency for people to react to events and incidents which further dilutes their sense of control. A former British prime minister was well

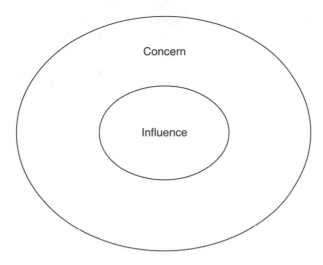

Figure 8.1 Circle of concern and circle of influence (Covey, 1989)

known for describing the most destabilising factors in his time as leader of the nation as 'events, dear boy, events'. So it must be for youth workers and others operating on the front line of public services as another policy directive swirls down from on high or yet another crisis hits a family or a community.

One writer on management (Covey, 1989) argues that effective people – whether leaders, managers or front-line staff – focus their attention and effort on things they can affect and in doing so tend to gain more influence. More reactive people are characterised as being more focused on the circle of concern. They may be unable to exercise any control over some of the problems and difficulties that affect them and then seek to blame others and avoid responsibility. If you are able to use your influence to expand into the circle of concern, you are more likely to have an impact on the complex and volatile situations you face and thereby increase your influence.

ACTIVITY *8.7*

- *How much control do you feel over your work?*
- *To what extent are you empowered to make key decisions?*
- *To what extent do you feel able to extend your area of influence and lessen your area of concern?*

Developing the skills of influence and persuasion

When you are working in a situation where you have no formal power, then you have to use whatever influence you can muster. In a multi-agency team you are likely to be one of several people who will each have a particular view of what might be the best way to intervene with a young person or a group of young people. If you think that a particular course of action may not be in the best interests of the young person or the group, you will then have to use your influencing skills in order to have your viewpoint listened to seriously and taken account of. This is influencing in order to persuade others.

There are other reasons why you may want to influence other people: to gain their support, to inspire them to give their best, to advocate on behalf of a group of young people, to win resources for a project, to co-operate with an organisation which can add value to the work you are doing.

Influencing skills require you to have a combination of the following:

- *self-awareness* – so you know your strengths and weaknesses, prejudices, the things that 'push your buttons' and upset you, your attitudes to people in authority;

- *interpersonal skills* – building a rapport with others, being open and direct, showing empathy and understanding, valuing and respecting what others can do, engendering trust;

- *communication* – clearly, concisely and enthusiastically, promising less and delivering more, reading the other person accurately, being an attentive and an active listener;

- *assertiveness* – being clear and confident, stating any differences with confidence and certainty, being consistent, standing your ground.

Building a rapport is an important first step in developing a strong position to influence. This means that you can help create a climate of trust and understanding. It also means that you can show you are on the same wavelength as others. Rapport is built by matching what others are doing without appearing to engage in imitation – 'the most sincere form of flattery'. Some people like to be flattered, others are made suspicious by it. If you can indicate that you see the world in a similar way and you have things in common, then that helps too. You can also build it by showing respect and understanding for the other's situation, but this has to be done with sincerity. The most convincing way to build rapport is to show that you are genuinely interested in the other person and how they see the world. You may not agree with the other's opinion but you can respect the other's right to hold and express it.

It helps to build rapport and develop your skills of influencing if you can reveal the values and impulses that drive you and discover those that drive the other, and if, in the words of St Francis of Assisi, you can 'seek to understand before seeking to be understood' – in other words make the other person feel their concerns have priority.

> *Thirty years ago negotiations between the Arabs and the Israelis over the Sinai desert had come to an impasse and a resolution was only found when the two major protagonists were encouraged to explore what the main drivers were for the other's position. In the peace talks at Camp David, President Sadat of Egypt and Prime Minister Begin of Israel made it clear that they each wanted control over the Sinai desert. When invited to share with each other why this disputed territory was so*

important, President Sadat explained that the driver behind his point of view was sovereignty because the land had always been Egypt's; whereas for Prime Minister Begin the issue was one of security because he saw the occupation of the territory as a threat to the borders of Israel. By sharing these differences, the seeds of eventual agreement were sown. The Sinai desert remained under Egyptian sovereignty and by agreeing that it would not be occupied Israel's need for security was satisfied. It proved possible to accommodate the two different drivers and each side felt they had gained some measure of assurance.

(Knight, 1995, p128)

In any negotiation there has to be some point at which alternatives to the preferred position can be considered. If neither party comes to the table with a best alternative, then they are not really serious about reaching agreement. In other words there should be some fall-back position which each side is prepared to adopt that will bring them closer than they would be without it. So if you are involved in a negotiation and are required to deploy your influencing skills, ensure that you come prepared to advance a different proposition from the one you begin with.

Furthermore, if you are seeking to influence the outcome of an argument or difference of view, then make sure you bring some evidence to support your position. Assertion followed by counter-assertion is probably going to end in frustration for both parties. Deadlock can sometimes be broken when assertion is illustrated and enhanced by evidence that substantiates the points being made. Clarity of analysis and argument buttressed by reliable evidence is usually sufficient to ensure that you can effectively influence the outcome.

ACTIVITY 8.8

- *How well honed are your influencing skills?*
- *Identify an example of a situation where you have successfully used them to secure the outcome you were seeking.*
- *How would you explain your success?*
- *Now identify an example when you used them without 'success'.*
- *What have you learned from that situation that you would seek to apply in others?*

C H A P T E R   R E V I E W

This chapter has discussed key priorities of policy about services for young people and identified some of the implications, emphasising government's concern:

- to ensure there are plenty of providers of young people's activities and services;
- that young people's voice is heard and they have a say about that provision;

- that decisions about services are made locally and that delivery is often neighbourhood based;

- that the services delivered and the workforce involved are more integrated.

The chapter has also identified some of the difficulties workers and managers face in dealing with this complexity and how best to maximise your influence for the benefit of young people.

FURTHER READING

Ford, K, Hunter, R, Merton, B and Waller, D (2005) *Leading and managing youth work and services for young people.* Leicester: The National Youth Agency.

Wood, J and Hines, J (eds) (2009) *Work with young people. Part two: policy and practice.* London: Sage.

McKimm, J and Philips, K (2009) *Leadership & management in integrated services.* Exeter: Learning Matters.

Knight, S (1995) *NLP at work.* London: Nicholas Brealey. See page 128.

USEFUL WEBSITES

CWDC integrated working section **www.cwdcouncil.org.uk/integrated-working**

REFERENCES

Children's Workforce Development Council (CWDC) (2008) *Integrated working explained.* Leeds: CWDC. Online: **www.cwdcouncil.org.uk/integrated-working-explained**

Covey, S (1989) *The seven habits of highly effective people.* London: Simon and Schuster.

Davies, B (1999a) *Voluntaryism to welfare state: a history of the youth service in England volume 1: 1939–1979.* Leicester: The National Youth Agency.

Davies, B (1999b) *Thatcherism to New Labour: a history of the youth service in England volume 2: 1979–1999.* Leicester: The National Youth Agency.

Davies, B (2008) *The New Labour years: a history of the youth service in England volume 3: 1997–2007.* Leicester: The National Youth Agency.

Davies, B and Merton, B (2009) *Squaring the circle.* Leicester: DMU. Online: **http://dmu.ac.uk/Images/Squaring%20the%20Circle_tcm6-50166.pdf**

Department for Education and Skills (2005) *Youth matters.* London: DfES.

Department for Education and Skills (2006) *Youth matters: the next steps.* London: DfES.

Department for Children, Schools and Families (2007) *Aiming high for young people: a ten-year strategy for positive activities.* London: DCSF.

Department for Children, Schools and Families (2008) *Statutory guidance on section 507B Education Act 1996*. London: DCSF.

Ford, K (2008) *Models of youth workforce leadership and management: a discussion document*. The NYA and FPM Training for the Children's Workforce Development Council.

Knight, S (1995) *NLP at work*. London: Nicholas Brealey.

McKimm, J and Held, S (2009) 'The emergence of leadership theory: from twentieth to the twenty-first century', in McKimm, J and Philips, K (eds) *Leadership & management in integrated services*. Exeter: Learning Matters.

Weaver, M (2006) More power to the people urges Miliband. *The Guardian*, 21 February. Online: **www.guardian.co.uk/society/2006/feb/21/localgovernment.politics**

Chapter 9
Conclusion

Mary Tyler

We set out to take a straightforward and practical approach through this book. This conclusion continues this approach and we hope it will help you reflect on the significance, scale and complexity of managing modern youth work, and the nature of the management role you have. We encourage you to consider where you are on your management journey and how well equipped you are for it. We also return to the issue of control and influence and encourage you to feel comfortable working with uncertainty. Whether it is a new excursion for you or one that is continuing, we hope you will finish this book with an enthusiasm and some fuel and equipment for this very important management journey.

Change, consistency and purpose

The preceding two chapters considered key aspects of English policy and the kinds of significant changes in the youth work field being driven by them. Whilst policy varies in other parts of the UK, the overall themes are similar. You will therefore be aware that managing youth work involves managing in the zone of complexity (see Chapter 8). Youth work is not alone in this. Many of the other human professions also face such change and complexity. Change and uncertainty are constants and you need to develop a capacity to cope with them. You also need to bear in mind that this is nothing new. The work environment is in a constant state of flux. Youth work has always adapted to change. For those who began practising youth work in the 1970s and 1980s, some of whom are managers today, it is a different world. Those managers have had to live with and make many changes. Young youth workers and young people have different life views in a global world so easily and profoundly connected through, for instance, travel and migration, global businesses, internet and mobile phone communication.

We now outline some of those changes and concerns and what this means for managing youth work today. There has never been a time when there has been such an emphasis on managing the quality of youth work because of current concerns about accountability and value for money. It has probably never mattered as much also that it is well managed, which includes enabling and ensuring its spontaneous qualities, working 'on the wing'. Youth work projects need to evidence results to maintain their credibility and hopefully their funding. Youth work is used in and visible now in many settings and alongside other professional contributions, especially through the development of IYSS in England. It is more valued not just because of its visibility but because of its ability to engage young people and, to a lesser extent, others in their communities in having a voice at a time when there is such a strong policy emphasis on citizenship and local decision making.

The professional identity of youth work is being challenged. It is perceived to be under threat, particularly in the English public sector context where it is increasingly located in integrated services and potentially drawn into working with those already labelled and targeted.

It is becoming more difficult to distinguish between public sector and voluntary sector provision as potentially more youth work is delivered by the voluntary sector commissioned by the public sector. You may wonder whether that matters. If more voluntary sector work is substantially dependent on public money with its prescriptive expectations, then there is a danger that youth work that starts from young people's direct interests and concerns will be compromised. However, there has been an increase in potentially more independent voluntary sector youth work in faith settings and provided by local communities (Jeffs and Smith, 2008).

These and other changes feature through the book and particularly in Chapters 1, 7 and 8. However, as Grey points out (2009), the current changes in the world are not necessarily any more significant than changes in the past, although they are different. Despite the changes of government, policy and funding and, for instance, the impact of recession, technological developments and globalisation, youth workers still find young people's aspirations and concerns are similar, such as getting a decent job and forming happy relationships. What they appreciate from youth work is fundamentally similar to the past – time, interest, care, respect, association, activities, personal development and fun (Davies and Merton, 2009). Youth work continues to make 'a considerable difference to their lives' (Merton et al., 2004, p6) as, for instance, they increase their confidence, make new friends, learn new skills and make their own decisions.

Managing youth work is about managing change and uncertainty, as well as managing consistency and certainty and therefore ensuring those consistent youth work features and benefits are maintained. As much as Bush (2008, p2) argues that 'educational management has to be centrally concerned with the purpose and aims of education', so youth work management has to be centrally and constantly concerned with the purpose and aims of youth work. Management has no meaning without being linked to the purpose of whatever it is managing.

This book has not attempted to examine the purpose and aims of youth work as many other books and literature do this, including a number of recent contributions (for instance, Young, 2005; Merton, 2007; Jeffs and Smith, 2008; Batsleer, 2008, Sapin, 2009; Wood and Hine, 2009). However, we will include here a very recent and UK-wide definition to remind you of youth work's overall intentions and values. It is from the QAA Youth and Community Work Benchmark Statement, which was developed for use by all the Higher Education Institutions who educate youth and community work students.

Youth and community work is a practice of informal and community education that involves the development of democratic and associational practices, which promote learning and development in the communities or individuals who choose to take part in the programmes that youth and community workers facilitate and support. It is focused on work with adolescents and adults, with groups as well as individuals, and with personal development in the context of the development of wider social networks and collective engagement with issues of social justice. Its pedagogic practice is based on the identification of and responses to needs and aspirations through dialogue and mutual aid.

(QAA, 2009, p9)

This book has been written at a time when there is a movement to revisit and 'defend' youth work indicated by numbers attending meetings at venues across England to debate the issue and take the opportunity to reflect critically on their work together. Those writing an 'open letter' on the subject describe youth work as 'volatile and voluntary, creative and collective – an association and conversation without guarantees' (Taylor, 2009, p1) which has been 'transformed . . . into an agency of behavioural modification' because of the government's concern 'with the micro-management of problematic, often demonised youth' (Taylor, 2009, p1).

Whilst this perspective is engaging people in positive debate, there are also signs of positive change. Both the current Labour government and the Conservative party, its potential successor, are moving away from the need for so many nationally identified targets for public services and placing increasing emphasis on community involvement in how services are delivered (Wintour and Watt, 2009). If you can keep your focus on the fundamentals of good youth work at this time, these should be the ideal driver of your practice as a new or experienced manager of modern youth work. In the next section we encourage you to reflect on your experience to date of youth work and its management before looking at what's needed to further develop your management competence.

The management development journey

ACTIVITY **9.1**

Our journeys are not all the same despite them having the youth work label.

- *How well are you doing your youth work now?*

- *How far have you come in your current job and in making it work for young people in that setting?*

- *Where do you want to take your youth work next?*

- *How well equipped are you for the managing modern youth work journey?*

- *At what stage are you on this journey? Are you just setting out?*

- *Were you on this management journey without fully recognising it? Have you been consciously navigating this journey for some time?*

When introducing ideas about how we learn to new youth work students, it has proved helpful to use the straightforward 'conscious competence' model of learning and development shown in Figure 9.1.

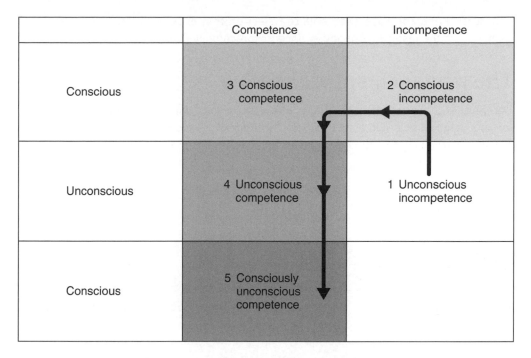

Figure 9.1 Conscious competence model of learning and development

Diagram based on and adapted from Chapman (2009)

This model is also useful for thinking about your competence in managing youth work.

1 Unconscious incompetence – you are unaware of what you don't know.

2 Conscious incompetence – you are aware of what you don't know.

3 Conscious competence – you know what you need to know and are consciously applying it to your management practice.

4 Unconscious competence – you are very familiar with what you need to know and usually apply it automatically and without awareness.

5 Consciously unconscious competence – you are able to consciously reflect on how you apply what you know and explain how you manage to others, and potentially support them in becoming consciously competent managers (a kind of learning about learning or meta learning). At this stage you are a reflective management practitioner.

What was your motivation for reading this book? Hopefully it has mapped out some significant aspects of what you need to manage modern youth work. Depending on your knowledge and experience to date of this work, you are now aware of what you need to learn (consciously incompetent) and you have achieved some learning (consciously competent). Alternatively you are reassured that much of this is familiar (unconsciously competent) and you have been able to reflect on that experience and add some ideas gained from the reading (consciously unconscious competence).

The management kit bag

Wherever you are on this managing youth work journey, you will need a body of knowledge, a range of skills and a set of values, attitudes and personal qualities. You also need a belief in your ability to influence and the skills to do so as discussed in the previous chapter and later in this one.

In terms of knowledge, we emphasise again that big picture understanding is crucially needed to manage modern youth work.

ACTIVITY 9.2

Return to Activity 2.1 about the concentric circles of people and organisations surrounding you and see what you would now add to it following further reading. If you have not undertaken it, turn to page 15 and begin the process. Develop a fuller map now of the many people, groups and organisations, and also the economic and policy influences on your youth work or the setting in which you work. You may find it valuable to use a model such as the PESTEL (e.g. Mullins, 2007, p87) or the similar TEMPLES model (e.g. Doherty and Horne, 2002, p70), which encourage you to identify the political, economic, socio-cultural, technological, environmental and legal influences many of which will originate in the outer circles.

So what about the role you play in this set of circles when managing youth work? How do you use your potential at the hub of this wheel positively (see Chapter 1) and avoid being at the beck and call of every new policy, manager and local elder. There are some practical tips later in this chapter about managing your boss and the boundaries of your work when faced with so many demands. Additionally, the previous chapter includes advice about dealing flexibly with complexity and not feeling you should always be in control of events.

Focusing specifically on your role, try thinking through the circumstances in which you are managing and identify the most suitable role to take. Recognise and understand the importance of playing a leadership role and also a management role. The leadership role is more responsive, about longer-term direction and has a focus on values. The management role is more reactive, about coordination and has a focus on performance management and effectiveness. To help you with this thinking, familiarise yourself with models of leadership, particularly the two key models of transactional and transformational leadership (e.g. Bush, 2003; Doherty and Horne, 2002). Transformational leadership 'emphasises inspiring and motivating people to do things for themselves' (Ford et al., 2005, p84) and is more change oriented. Transactional leadership is the more traditional planning, organising and controlling and is more order oriented (McKimm and Phillips, 2009). The balance of the management and leadership roles you play in each post you fill is different. The same post at different times demands a different balance too. When you are, for instance, establishing a new project and work approaches, you need to play more to a vision, lead the way hopefully in an appropriately consultative manner. If you are managing work with a settled and experienced team and wanting to maintain and raise the quality, you may be playing more of a management or transactional role.

Understand your place in the middle at the hub of these circles of Activity 9.2, facing both up and down inside your organisation and also around the inside and outside your organisation. You need to understand the stakeholders you are in contact with and their range of perspectives, some of which maybe very different from your own. Rather than dismiss or ignore them, you need the knowledge to understand why there are such different and sometimes negative views in order to challenge stakeholders' assumptions on, for instance, young people in general or a particular issue such as teenage parents. This could lead to you negotiating and constructing a different role for youth work with such groups. Be supportive of the pressures and responsibilities young parents experience and ensure they can engage with opportunities that enable their further development. However, ensure youth workers are seen to have a role that challenges the negative stereotypes and assumptions that being a young parent is bad news, which bystanders often believe and which are often internalised by the parents themselves. Achieve an understanding in key stakeholders that youth work has a particular contribution to make which is about enabling young parents to develop and promote positive images of themselves and their achievements and to participate in opportunities to influence policy and practice.

Make sure you know what's happening on your doorstep. Know the youth work you manage and what is being achieved. Know your team and the area, the detailed picture inside the big picture.

Of course knowledge and understanding are only a starting point. To manage you need skills too. A very significant aspect of management is about working with people and encouraging them to produce high-quality work and supporting their development. Youth workers should have the necessary skills for this given that building trusting developmental relationships is central to their work of supporting young people to meet their needs and aspirations. Youth workers should have good levels of emotional intelligence which will be valuable as managers. They are also used to, for instance, handling conflict, challenge and creativity and planning activities and projects with young people. Youth workers learn to deliver planned sessions and also react to situations and concerns and work spontaneously. Management also involves both planned and emergent strategies and good management practice includes organisational debate about change and improvement (see organisational learning Chapter 3).

A range of skills have been covered in this book.

- Communication from the various positions that youth work managers hold including leading, acting as buffer in the middle, ensuring the reputation of youth work.

- Supporting and developing staff so they can do a good job by providing clear expectations, a constructive supportive climate and regular supervision. There will potentially be more opportunity for innovation and experimentation as government recognises explicitly the difficulty of doing so if services are busy ticking boxes. There is now a reduced emphasis on national targets as a way of further improving public services (Byrne, 2009).

• Developing local targets with local people, selecting ones that are suitable for your current team and its skills and designed with current structures in mind. Then revising them regularly to keep them relevant and achievable and to ensure they are helpful guides and do not become ends in themselves.

• Evidencing the work and also broadcasting and promoting it in and outside your organisation.

• Networking – being at the right tables and building alliances with partners. Find sources of support and opportunities to share good practice such as group supervision with peers in your part of the country.

To apply the necessary knowledge and these kinds of skills effectively, you need a very clear sense of direction and purpose. Your attitudes and values are central to this. The approach and attitude you take, the qualities you need and the values reinforcing your work are like the words through a stick of seaside rock and the main focus at this stage of this book. At whatever level you manage, 'the ability of the public service worker to act independently, with courage, conviction, and on the basis of a public service ethos, is critical' (Haynes, 2003, p155). You need this commitment to improving the lives of those who miss out in this society in your mind, emotions and actions. You also need integrity, tenacity and realism.

Manage critically using a sharp and reflective approach informed by your values as discussed in Chapter 1. Do not forget the values, it is not just about getting the right supplies in your kitbag of management resources. Such skills and techniques Watson would argue are not 'neutral and "innocent" in a political sense' (2006, p13). They need to be used to ensure good youth work that benefits young people and in the context of many of them being demonised and disadvantaged in our society.

Develop a positive attitude to change. 'A glass half full' perspective will help. For instance, as a youth worker you look for the potential of young people, so see the potential of youth work in your context. Believe in youth work's contribution and in your ability to make it. This way you can do something about achieving it. For instance, expect and encourage creativity that can emerge from the mix of professional backgrounds and skills coming together in many integrated settings. You can do this either as team manager or peer. Believe in human agency, in the ability of people to make choices despite the pressures from all the things in those concentric circles. Naturally with this comes a belief in yourself and your team.

Prioritise trust. Gaining the trust of others in you, and trusting colleagues and those you manage, particularly where more youth workers are in virtual teams and teams with other professionals. Trusting partners by spending time together – gain and maintain involvement and support from other agencies for the work you do as well as contributing to their agendas.

Be comfortable in living with ambiguity and uncertainty. In fact exploit it. Good youth work has often been associated with creativity and grabbing opportunities as they arise.

Do not feel all that you manage has to be controlled. Be happy to keep working it out and do not assume there is necessarily a solution that management theory has traditionally led us to believe is the case. 'Managers who can learn to embrace the unknown, and to relish uncertainty, will thrive in organizations where these attributes are in short supply' (Doherty and Horne, 2002, p31). The management of contemporary public service change means 'managing the relatively unmanageable' (Wallace et al., 2007, p1); however, 'people based at different levels of public service systems do cope with the complexity of change, one way or another, despite their inherently limited capacity for control' (Wallace et al., 2007, p2).

Be assertive about youth work's contribution and confident about the influence you can have in these changing times. Youth work can potentially be more influential now as a result of its more central position alongside contributions of other professionals to young people's lives.

Take some responsibility for your development as a manager of modern youth work. How do you think you measure up against the contents of this kitbag of skills, knowledge, values, qualities and attitudes? What could you do to develop your management competence? Reading this book and continuing to use it and other relevant reading will be a good starting point. Other developmental activities and experiences include getting regular critical feedback through conversations of various types with peers; good regular supervision and appraisal; training; observation of others' management practice; talking with colleagues about their practice; and engaging in action learning sets about demands and dilemmas you face in managing youth work (McGill and Brockbank, 2004).

Control and influence

Control and influence has been a theme running through this book and has been illustrated in a number of ways. As we reach the end we look briefly close to home.

At any level in your organisation perhaps one of the key people you need to learn how to manage is your boss, usually your line manager, sometimes members of a committee. This may sound back to front. But in a productive relationship there has to be give and take and it is important that you are not slavishly and persistently answering to your boss's beck and call and that you feel instead some measure of independence, autonomy and control. A good line manager will recognise this and give you a fair degree of licence to work in the way that suits your style and the demands of the situation where you are located. She will know less about your work than you do so make sure she hears about it. That way you can have some influence.

Some managers can be too controlling and others can be neglectful, in the latter case intervening only at points where they think you have transgressed in some way or other. Yet others may delegate work to you at the last minute or delegate then interfere or change their requests. You can help your boss improve as a manager by making reasonable demands, ensuring that you have regular meetings to discuss the work and for professional supervision and that these are properly recorded. You can use your influencing skills to ensure that your manager lets you play to your strengths, express your creativity and use your enterprise and initiative. And it is important that you do not let your boss dump on you any of their own anxieties or simply push in your direction any tasks they do not want to do themselves. It is important that you remain firm and that your manager is required to observe and maintain boundaries in the same way that you do.

Managing boundaries is the essence of all good youth work. In the same way that an effective youth worker helps young people to recognise boundaries and behave appropriately in response, so you have to manage boundaries in your work. This is especially so when operating in a complex policy environment where service managers are being required to join things up and, in a sense, erode boundaries.

There is clearly a tension here and it is not easy to resolve. A common complaint among youth workers in the current climate is not only that they are being called upon to do too much with too little but that they are also asked to do too many different things and they feel pulled in different directions and answerable to too many stakeholders with sometimes what appear to be competing interests. Confused? You have the right to be!

While flexibility in a service is usually regarded as a virtue, there is a narrow line between being flexible and being manipulated. As someone once said, 'If I always say "yes", what is my "no" worth?'

The bottom line is that as a youth worker you keep asking the question 'How does this – what you are asking me to do – actually benefit the young people I am working with? And what are you asking me to stop doing in order to do it?' If you cannot get a satisfactory answer from your line manager, you have a case and can reasonably make a challenge.

This is not to advocate dissent, only clarity, consistency and reasonableness of expectation. If it is not provided, the chances are that the service you provide for young people will be impaired. Young people deserve the best opportunities and your job is to do what you can to secure them. Managing yourself effectively is a crucial first step. Early in this book's journey we looked at this so it has come full circle.

Managing modern youth work is hard, complex, stressful work but it should also be exciting, engaging and provide plenty of job satisfaction.

C H A P T E R   R E V I E W

This last chapter has emphasised again the need for clear direction and purpose to ensure your management work is benefiting young people's lives. In doing this it has:

- reminded you that managing youth work involves managing change and uncertainty and also maintaining the consistency of youth work's key features;

- encouraged you to review your level of management competence and use your management role clearly and positively;

- outlined some key knowledge, skills, values and personal qualities you need to have positive influence and to lead good youth work.

FURTHER READING

Ford, K, Hunter, R, Merton, B and Waller, D (2005) *Leading and managing youth work and services for young people.* Leicester: The National Youth Agency.

McKimm, J and Phillips, K (eds) (2009) *Leadership and management in integrated services.* Exeter: Learning Matters.

REFERENCES

Batsleer, J (2008) *Informal learning in youth work.* London: Sage.

Bush, T (2003) *Theories of educational leadership and management.* 3rd edition. London: Sage.

Bush, T (2008) *Leadership and management development in education.* London: Sage.

Byrne, L (2009) *Today* programme, BBC Radio 4 interview, 27 June. Online: **http://news.bbc.co.uk/today/hi/today/newsid_8122000/8122094.stm**

Chapman, A (2009) *Conscious Competence Learning* model. Online: **www.businessballs.com/consciouscompetencelearningmodel.htm**

Davies, B and Merton, B (2009) *Squaring the circle.* Online: **http://dmu.ac.uk/Images/Squaring%20the%20Circle_tcm6-50166.pdf**

Doherty, T and Horne, T (2002) *Managing public services.* London: Routledge.

Ford, K, Hunter, R, Merton, B and Waller, D (2005) *Leading and managing youth work and services for young people.* Leicester: The National Youth Agency.

Grey, C (2009) *A very short, fairly interesting and reasonably cheap book about studying organisations.* 2nd edition. London: Sage.

Haynes, P (2003) *Managing complexity in the public services.* Berkshire: Open University Press.

Jeffs, T and Smith, M (2008) 'Valuing youth work', *Youth & Policy*, 100: 277–302.

McGill, I and Brockbank, A (2004) *The action learning handbook.* London: RoutledgeFalmer.

McKimm, J and Phillips, K (eds) (2009) *Leadership and management in integrated services.* Exeter: Learning Matters.

Merton, B (2007) *Good youth work: what youth workers do, why and how.* Leicester: National Youth Agency.

Merton, B, Payne, M and Smith, D (2004) *An evaluation of the impact of youth work in England.* Research Report 606. Nottingham: DfES Publications.

Mullins, LJ (2007) *Management and organisational behaviour.* 8th edition. Harlow: Financial Times/ Prentice Hall (or earlier editions).

Quality Assurance Agency (2009) *Subject benchmark statement: youth and community work.* Gloucester: QAA. Online: **www.qaa.ac.uk/academicinfrastructure/benchmark/statements/YouthandCommunity09.pdf**

Sapin, K (2009) *Essential skills for youth work practice.* London: Sage.

Taylor, T (2009) *The in defence of youth work letter.* Online:

http://indefenceofyouthwork.wordpress.com/the-in-defence-of-youth-work-letter/

Wallace, M, Fertig, M and Schneller, E (2007) *Managing change in the public services.* Oxford: Blackwell.

Watson, TJ (2006) *Organising and managing work.* 2nd edition. Harlow: Financial Times/ Prentice Hall.

Wintour, P and Watt, N (2009) 'Labour ready to abandon Tony Blair's public service targets', *The Guardian* 26 June. Online: **www.guardian.co.uk/politics/2009/jun/26/labour-public-service-targets**

Wood, J and Hine, J (eds) (2009) *Work with young people: theory and policy for practice.* London: Sage.

Young, K (2006) *The art of youth work.* 2nd edition. Dorset: Russell House Publishing.

Index